DO YOU
BELIEVE?

DO YOU BELIEVE?

92 Miracles So Far and Counting!
RICH MASON

Trilogy Christian Publishers

A Wholly Owned Subsidary of Trinity Broadcasting Network

2442 Michelle Drive

Tustin, CA 92780

For information, address Trilogy Christian Publishing

Rights Department, 2442 Michelle Drive, Tustin, Ca 92780.

Trilogy Christian Publishing/ TBN and colophon are trademarks of Trinity Broadcasting Network.

For information about special discounts for bulk purchases, please contact Trilogy Christian Publishing.

Manufactured in the United States of America

10 9 8 7 6 5 4 3 2 1

Library of Congress Cataloging-in-Publication Data is available.

ISBN 978-1-68556-302-8

ISBN 978-1-68556-303-5 (ebook)

Dedication

This book is dedicated to my wife, Beckie, who has been by my side throughout this entire journey; without God bringing us together, I would have been a very different man. Thank you for the love, laughter, support, adventure, and joy you brought to our lives over the past thirty-four years. I truly thank God for you; you are awesome.

And to our three wonderful children, all fearfully and wonderfully made, with great plans that God has for you: thank you for the joy you bring to our lives. I hope this book clears up why your parents are crazy for Jesus in a good way.

To my father, who taught me the value of a life lived well through his unwavering consistency, his uncompromising integrity, and the limitless potential that comes from diligent hard work and perseverance: thank you for the solid foundation, Dad. It will be a joy to be all together in glory one day.

And finally, to my mother, who is still thinking about nurturing and caring for her children at ninety-four years of age, even while we all try to care for her: thank you for modeling love and caring, Mom.

Table of Contents

Introduction

With the heart of a father, I pray this book encourages you, strengthens you, and trains you for your journey so that you will live your life to the full by living your life full of faith. That is, faith in the One who can impress you with something new, amazing, and great every time!

What I didn't know then, but I know now, is that it begins with, it is infused throughout with, and it will ultimately end with love. So, I would be negligent not to tell you *that* here in the beginning. It is the most incredible and amazing story, and the one question that sets an entire life in a completely new direction and into an overwhelming part in this love story of the universe is this: Do you believe?

What comes next is not just my story, my tiny drop of water in this massive ocean, but a small take at the full story God tells from the perspective of an average person (me) and many other people encountering the undeniable.

And just like a child playing in a mud puddle in the backyard, getting his or her brightly colored bathing suit dirty while waiting for his or her mom and dad to get everything ready to go to the beach, so we have an enormous spiritual beach to enjoy. Getting to the enormous spiritual beach requires finding out we're not on the greatest of waterfront property right now, in the mud puddle, and we're not enjoying what is fully and readily available to all, regardless of circumstances, origins, socioeconomic status, appearance, history, or anything. I suggest you read this and react appropriately not to miss the beach by staying playing in the puddle!

NEW YEAR'S RESOLUTION

Looking across the flat water, I can see a boat three miles offshore, just sitting there. We've been in this house for over two weeks now, and it's been there the whole time. We haven't seen anyone come or go to the shore, and our view is right out across the water and beautiful—thank You, Lord!

It's been quite a wild ride to get here, not just to this fantastic view on the water, not just back to Florida from across the country. Let me explain:

In 2002, I was working for a semiconductor company as an international sales manager, covering the Southeast of the US and South America as my two main geographic territories. I was laid off in the economic downturn after the 9/11 attacks on the US twin towers. As I prayed about what God wanted us to do, I felt Him lead us to something huge and quite scary. I mean huge, risky, and very scary!

We had all three of our children at that time, and the youngest, Elijah, was just turning three. (He's twenty-one now. Wow, I can't believe how time flies!) Elijah would play right outside my closed den doors and tap on the glass, wanting to play with me. Many times, I would think, *Do you know how busy I am? I'm trying to make something happen here.*

You know how that is, don't you? Me! I was going to make something happen. Not really—I had no money, no influence, no power, no patents, no advantages, other than the one advantage that takes care of everything: I know the God who owns everything and holds the universe together! Just like when I knew someone or something was orchestrating things all around me: I can explain that too, but to do so, allow me to go back further in time, to the year 1996.

I'm working for Rockwell Semiconductor Systems as a sales engineer, and the purse of my wife, Beckie, gets stolen out of a McDonald's playroom. She's there with our special-needs daughter, and the purse is just suddenly gone. We reported it to the police, and eventually, they found a young teen who had taken it. A month or so previously, there was the first schoolyard shooting back then: not Columbine, this was Arkansas somewhere, and I had made a New Year's resolution to do something about this horrible new kids-shooting-kids thing. You see, I grew up in New York City, so I've seen and experienced urban problems, let's just call them, firsthand. But aside from a gang shooting, no one had ever gone into a school and just shot other kids. Kids shooting kids? Never!

Now, if you're younger than I am, you might not quite get that, so let me repeat it. Never! It never happened in my lifetime that I had ever heard of! No kid would take a gun into a school and randomly shoot other kids. We may have had a lot of shootings since then, but you need to hear that this was the first. That's why a strong something began inside my belly.

I didn't normally make New Year's resolutions, but we had the neighbors over on New Year's Eve, and Pauline from next door asked, "Who's got a resolution?" So, when it was my turn, I surprised myself and said something like, "I don't know what's going on with this schoolyard shooting, but that is not good. Some things gotta be done, and I'm going to do something about it!" I'm sure someone said something like, "Good for you," and we all got another beer or champagne. Me! I was going to do something! Ha, I couldn't do a thing. Oh, I tried, and trust me: I'm an overachiever engineer, so when I go after something, I usually go 110 percent. I only have two speeds: full-speed pedal to the metal or parked.

So, I went to work, trying to find out how to help kids. But everywhere I tried, I ran into a dead end. However, each time I tried a front door, a side door would open that I didn't even think of.

I'll give you an example: How do you help youth that are having such problems that it makes them want to steal some mother's purse while she's struggling to take care of a special child that needs extra care in many, many ways? Easy: you go to juvenile justice, right? Just try calling the local courthouse or the department of juvenile justice. I got nowhere but phone jail! I got answering machines, and I got put on hold, and I got "push one for directions; push two for the administrative offices..." Zippo!

But when they found the kid that took Beckie's purse, they sent us a letter asking if it was okay for him to do community service instead of giving back the money. At the bottom of that letter were the name and number of a probation-officer type, someone from juvenile justice—side door! I called the number and got connected.

I asked them, "What if a guy like me wanted to help out juveniles? Am I allowed to help?"

They said, "Of course!"

Boom, side door! Just like that, I went in through a side door, and you won't believe what happened next.

DO YOU REALLY WANT TO KNOW?

The Department of Juvenile Justice, district five, had a group where people could help kids. There were so many of those "you won't believe what happened next" experiences (side doors) that it's hard to believe. The department had a group called the Faith Community Network, a group of people from different organizations. Some were church groups, and some were organizations with drug-addiction recovery services, and some were judges, and some were police officers, all trying to help. I joined them as just a guy who wanted to help. And after a short time, they ended up asking me to lead the group (side door). The Lord always seems to do that with me. He has given me a knack for organizing things at the highest level—I call it the framework—so that the organization or project is optimized for its goals. I don't think it's that difficult, but God keeps putting me in places He wants me to lead and colead (more on that later).

As the leader of the group and as an engineer, I needed to start with the entire-requirements list: to help youth, we needed to know the top items youth needed help with. I asked every person in our group for the top three, and one item bubbled up as a major contributor or root cause on everyone's list: youth needed family help. I asked the people from the addiction services, "What's the top item?" They answered, "Their family." I asked the judge; he said, "Family." I asked the arresting officers; they said, "Family." Almost all troubled youth come from families that have deep, huge problems. A broken or terribly struggling family might lead to the drug problem or the desperation that led to theft, or the lack of love/support/guidance from parents might lead to gang support. Suddenly, I had a path to make a significant difference in the lives of youth: we just needed to create the right process that brings help for youth's families. *It may be that simple*, I thought.

I wondered why no one ever thought of this. Quickly, I had a bit of a framework in mind to help. Somehow, the woman in charge of Juvenile Justice, district five (our district), asked me if I wanted to run my family-program framework idea by the assistant state attorney: she could set it up (side door).

The three of us sat in the Applebee's on East Lake Road: Jill from district five, Juvenile Justice, and Barbara, assistant state attorney to Harry Lee Cole. I told Barbara my idea to help youth's families; she said something like, "It'll never happen: no senator wants anyone in his or her business just because their kid smoked pot; they'll never vote for it."

"Okay," I said, "How about this? [think: an engineer designing a solution] We take it to the extreme: how about three felonies by age thirteen, and we get to check the family, not for crimes, but for what help they need to thrive?"

Barbara said, "That might work, but let me ask you a question: you're an engineer; you just started going to the church you're attending [for the kids, not for me: I understood life, but it was to get our children some morals, or so I thought!]; what do you know about family programs?"

I thought for a few seconds about all the side doors, and I said, "All I know is help will be provided!" Then I looked over her shoulder and saw a man walking in the door, and I continued by saying, "And here he comes now!"

Of course, she turned around to look at who I was referring to, and he said, "Barbara!" and she called his name (Jack). "What are you doing these days?" he asked, and Barbara said, "I'm the assistant state attorney for Harry Lee Cole. What are you doing? Are you still pastoring that church in Fort Lauderdale?" "No," he said, "now I help churches create family programs."

Our mouths dropped open, and one of us said, "Then, I, uh, guess you'll want, eh, his phone number."

I couldn't believe what had just happened! How did I know this person walking in the door could create family programs? More importantly to me: How did I know to say it? Why did I say it? What made him walk in right at that time? Can someone orchestrate all these things at one time and then give me words to say? I was floored!

When I got home, I looked up at the wall of my room. I said, "God? Uh, are You really there?"

He answered me, not in my ears, but resonating inside my head and my heart or something. He said, "Do you really want to know?"

I knew what He meant: Are you ready to know that I'm here, that I have always been, that I see everything? My heart was beating out of my chest, but I was more than ready this time. To explain this "this time," I have to go back again, much further back, twenty years or so earlier than that, to when I was about twelve years old. It's only now that I can connect all of these events throughout my life!

It must have been a weekend because my older brothers were out somewhere. My parents were next door, I think, at the neighbor's house, visiting. I was watching a movie on TV about the Bible; I honestly can't remember if it was *King of Kings* or *The Ten Commandments*. All I remember is I was captivated by a sense of God, that He was watching over me. As the movie ended, I got off the couch to go upstairs, and I was saying to myself, "Show me the light." I'm not sure why I was saying that sentence instead of something like "God, can You please appear to me?" but that's what I meant by it. I meant, "God, please appear to me," but I walked toward the steps saying, "Show me the light," and went up the steps, saying it out loud. And I meant it! I really wanted Him to appear to me. I knew He was there; I sensed Him somehow. I can't really explain how I knew He was there with me, around me, everywhere, huge and caring.

But then it happened: it got lighter! He started to show me light! The staircase upstairs was dark, and no lights were on upstairs either, so when He started to show me light, I got scared out of my wits. I ran to the light switch and popped it on, saying, "Never mind, never mind: don't show me; don't show me." I was so scared; I wasn't ready—that time. This is the *first miracle* that I can remember.

But then, twenty-two years later, I was still scared but ready to at least find out who God was. I had no idea what was about to happen, and my heart beat out of my chest when He said into my insides, "Do you really want to know?"

I thought about how He just orchestrated a person coming into the Applebee's, having just the right qualifications, and speaking out through me. (I'll call this *miracle two* if you discount all the side doors.) Of course, I said yes to God, and something inside me changed. I didn't feel anything physical, not like a tingle or anything that I can describe, but something happened, and I knew it. I just didn't know what it was yet (*miracle three*). But I knew, right then, I would have to find out.

I then knew there really is a God; He just opened a bunch of side doors, talked out through me, and orchestrated events so that a guy who did family programs arrived while we were having a lunch meeting about youth, and the solution of it all was about family programs. What I didn't know was, do we just do whatever we did at Applebee's? Some sort of communicating in my head and heart? Or is there more? Is it the Bible? How could it be? I knew I needed to find out and knew where to start.

We were already going to First United Methodist Church of Tarpon Springs; they had a neat Christmas tree of people up on their stage (or altar?). So, I began the rest of my journey there by asking and listening carefully to the people who seemed to have something; they seemed to have a combination of passion and a sense of caring for people. Not just their own clique of friends—we saw plenty of that, unfortunately. But this group of leaders didn't seem to do things to be noticed or to get credit; in fact, it was quite the opposite: the things I noticed, and I was watching carefully, they did whether there was a crowd or no one else there.

Like the children's minister Sylvia Ragsdale. She would stoop down and tell an eight-year-old boy, "You're gonna do great! God has a purpose and a destiny for your life!" She didn't do it to impress the parents because I watched her do it when no one else was there; she didn't know I was there. And she seemed to mean it; "a specific destiny!" she would say. When she said stuff, something in my heart would go, "Yes, that sounds right!"

One day, I decided to sit in again during her children's church to see how our son was doing and what they were being taught (protective dad). In the end, she prayed something that really got my attention. She said, "I pray not only for these children but also for all of the parents and helpers here that they would all meet You, Lord Jesus! That You would reveal Yourself to them, and Father, I pray You would grant them salvation, all of them, young and old, that they would surrender to You and receive the forgiveness of sins You purchased out of love, at the cross, in Jesus's name. Amen!"

I thought, *What does that all mean? There's so much there!* I grew up in the Orthodox Church, and most of that seemed to be about following a ceremony. Sit down, stand up, say this, sing that, walk here, take some bread, done.

I mean no disrespect to the Orthodox part of the body of Christ: this was my impression of my experiences as a boy. As David said, *"The Lord forbid that I should do such a thing to my master, the Lord's anointed, or lay my hand on him; for he is the anointed of the Lord"* (1 Samuel 24:6).

But this: What was this? Meet Jesus? He can reveal Himself? The Father grants salvation?

In engineering fashion, I began to take note of all the details. I had so many questions: Where did she get this? How can she say it with such confidence? What is the source of her confidence? And how does she know? Where is the "data sheet" with the details? And how does anyone know it's reliable with that much confidence? Then, I asked her! And so it began…

A few months before this, after playing basketball with my colleagues from Paradyne, we went out for a beer and a burger to a local place called the Varsity Club. For some reason, we all violated social norms (because we were just a bunch of friends) and began to talk about politics and religion.

About religion, someone said, "I don't understand why a murdering slimebag could ask for forgiveness on his last dying breath and get forgiven, while we try to live good lives! That doesn't sound right to me: Why would God do that?"

Just then, a brave guy walking by asked, "Guys, do you mind if I take a crack at that question?" We're friendly people, so we said, "Sure, have at it!" Then this guy, named Theo, took the salt and pepper shakers and laid them out on the table. He put one to the left and said, "Let's suppose this saltshaker represents the best person on the earth, maybe Mother Teresa? And the pepper shaker way over here, to the right, is the worst murdering slimebag. You guys are somewhere in the middle." And we laughed and joked about who was way over toward the slimebag and who wasn't. He continued, "The problem is God is way over in California [remember we're in Florida, so that's pretty far off the table], and none of us can get there from here because we have all sinned. And God can't be with sin. So, anyone who gets to be with God gets there because of Jesus, who is the bridge from here to California and the way to have our sins removed or forgiven forever!"

One guy, Chappy, piped up, "Do you have courtroom-worthy evidence to prove that Jesus actually died for our sins? My wife's an attorney, so I know courtroom-worthy!" And Theo said, "Absolutely, there's a ton of evidence. I can show you the many books on many subjects." Chappy jumped back in, "If it's courtroom-worthy, I should be able to interview them and cross-examine them right here, right now!" And he pounded his finger pointing to the table. Chappy's a good man, and I'm sure he was just making a legal point. Another friend of mine, Don Snoll, was there too that night. "Snollster," as I call him, is a good man and a good friend.

Theo calmly said, "I can't bring people here from 2,000 years ago, but there's a ton of evidence, including eyewitness evidence and opposition evidence [meaning: the people who were opposed]. If anyone wants to see it, I can give you my phone number."

As Theo said that, something inside me pinged, just a little bit. It was like a small bell hit one "ping." Like in the movie *The Hunt for Red*

October with Sean Connery. The captain said, "Reverify our range to target, one ping only."

I looked back over my shoulder (Theo was talking behind me this whole time) and said, "I'll take your number." So, he wrote his name and number on the little tear-off piece that used to be at the bottom of the restaurant checks, and I folded it and stuffed it into my wallet for another time, half wondering why I said yes.

I think that's why this "seed" of searching began to grow inside me. I started wondering, *Is there evidence? How much evidence? Maybe it's actually possible to know, for certain, about all of this?* With this seed of searching beginning to grow, I had to find out more, much more.

PROVE IT TO ME!

One of my next questions to Sylvia was, "You claim all these things are in the Bible, but how do you know the Bible is true and even the same as originally intended? Wasn't it written many years ago and passed down for generations? We could tell a secret in a circle of ten people right now, and it wouldn't even come back the same!"

Her answer intrigued me; she said, "I've always just known the Bible to be true—all my life! But if you need proof, then you should talk to Paul; he did some research." She was that nonchalant about it.

Of course, I went to Paul. Paul couldn't recall much that was convincing, but he pointed me to a book called *Evidence That Demands a Verdict* by Josh McDowell. Now, that sounded more like what I was looking for! I read that book, and it had some great evidence in it, although it was written in a very hard-to-read format for me. It has since been reformatted, thankfully.

But I needed more. I wanted someone to also refute the evidence because what did I know about ancient Rome? I'm not a history expert, and I needed someone who didn't have an agenda. In fact, I wanted someone who was totally against Christianity (the opposition) to give me their best reasons against it.

When you want to know what's wrong with a Chevy, you don't ask Chevy. You ask Ford! Then you can ask Chevy what's good about a Chevy, that's your *min* and your *max*, as we call it in engineering, when we're dealing with specifications (sorry for going there—habit!).

Then I found it: the Ford against the Chevy! There's this guy Lee Strobel who was the legal editor for the *Chicago Tribune*, so he's a smart dude, an attorney, and I assume he's been around a lot of different types of people, events, organizations, and political people. It turns out his wife becomes a Christian, and he's upset; he thinks she's gone bonkers like some of the religious nuts he's written about in the newspaper. She says, "This is not religion; this is Jesus Christ!" "Same thing," he says, "I'll prove it to you," which launches him to try to disprove Christianity! That's what I wanted: show me your best information against it!

He goes right for the heart of Christianity, the resurrection! Did this Jesus guy actually rise from the dead? With no resurrection, Christianity wouldn't even be a club; it would be worthless. So, Strobel goes for three simple but powerful things: "First, prove to me Jesus was dead! Maybe He wasn't even dead—there's this whole swoon theory—maybe He just passed out. Second, prove to me He was buried. And number three: prove to me He was seen alive. Because if there's a guy who was certifiably dead and was then seen alive, that'd be enough for even a skeptic like me!" Strobel said.

So, I guess because he's a newspaper guy and has money and connections and resources, he flies (remember: before COVID-19, we used to fly on planes without masks!) to see experts, and, bottom line, he proves it beyond a shadow of a doubt. He proves the dead guy got up! Read it for yourself: Strobel has one book called *The Case for Easter* with just those three chapters. He has another book called *The Case for Christ*, where he covers over ten different categories of evidence, proving Christianity. You can't read this detail with an open mind and not conclude Jesus is real and alive and the Bible is really God's written and protected word.

I'll give you just one of the many topics. Do you know how we decide an ancient book is historically accurate? We must see multiple copies. It must be copies because the old paper deteriorated, so people had to constantly make handwritten copies. We have to see multiple copies, actually pieces of copies (called manuscripts) from different geographic areas, which have no agenda of their own. If there's a bunch of copies from different areas with no agenda, we call it a historically accurate book; we conclude it was really written a long time ago and we have a valid copy of what the original was.

The second most historically accurate book is Homer's *Iliad*. It has copies from different areas, with no agenda, and there are about 500 different fragments/copies that we've found—that's a lot!

Do you know what book is number one? Yes, the Bible! There are over 5,000 fragments, copies (manuscripts) of just the Greek translation alone! That's a book that has ten times the amount of the closest book, and that's just the Greek translation!

Josh McDowell's *Evidence That Demands a Verdict* book describes why this is; by the way, it's because to be a Jewish scribe was a way of life. You would start out at some young age (I think about nine years old or so) and would shadow a real scribe; you would dress like him, eat like him, do everything he did. And a scribe would not look up, even in the presence of a king (which in those days meant a death sentence), if he was in the middle of copying the Word of God! That's how seriously they took copying the Word of God!

There are tons of great evidence in just those two books, but I've checked many, many other books, of course (see the partial book list at the end). Here are the topics Lee Strobel investigated in just one, *The Case for Christ*, book:

- The Eyewitness Evidence
- The Documentary Evidence (we just talked about some of this)
- The Corroborating Evidence
- The Scientific Evidence
- The Rebuttal Evidence
- The Identity Evidence
- The Psychological Evidence
- The Profile Evidence
- The Fingerprint Evidence
- The Medical Evidence
- The Evidence of the Missing Body
- The Evidence of Appearances
- The Circumstantial Evidence

I had a college professor who said if you can't talk about a subject, starting with the general and going down to the specific and then back up to the general again, you don't know the subject well. That has encouraged part of my personality whereby I almost always start analysis at the general level. In other words, starting with the basics or the fundamentals or the high-level view.

From my digging and researching, I found the following compelling high-level pieces of evidence: if you look up at the sky, there is no doubt someone or something designed that. There's just no way of looking at burning balls of gas and other things in the sky that are always there in perfectly synchronized orbits and not knowing someone designed it. If you dive into any level deeper, you will find even more amazement at the intentional design that is required as it moves much further and further away from any possibility of chance or random circumstance.

Just look at our own solar system with our sun. It is ninety-one million miles away, or eight light minutes. Things are so big in space that we have to measure them using the distance light travels for a certain time. Now, our sun is in *the* perfect position so that the gravitational pull keeps the earth from flying out into space and freezing and the rotational momentum keeps the earth from being pulled into the sun and completely burning up. With our one solar system and our one sun, we are but a tiny speck of sand on a beach of other solar systems: millions of these burning-balls-of-gas-based solar systems are in our one Milky Way galaxy. And there are millions of galaxies! Yet, they are all in perfect positions, so we can know what stars were visible in our earth's sky on any day back in history. They are that synchronized! That's not random; that's amazingly designed and synchronized!

And what about the earth? Have you ever seen the trees in fall change color? Who does that? And everyone knows the trees take in carbon dioxide and give off oxygen, but it's still a pretty cool design to provide oxygen, isn't it? Sometimes, while I'm hunting, as the darkness turns to dawn, the stunning view of the surrounding area mountains and valley plays an amazing song to the eyes that tells of Him. Amazing! And did you ever stop to think how food comes up out of the earth? These are high-level concepts where you can see with your eyes that there is a definite design.

What if we start to look a little deeper? Did you know that the earth is protected from the sun's high-energy light by a three-tiered system in our atmosphere? As it turns out, nitrogen has a triple bond holding two molecules together. It takes the highest-energy gamma rays to break the triple bond, so the harmful gamma rays from our sun use up their energy and don't harm us. The remaining nitrogen is good fertilizer! The medium harmful X-rays from our sun use up their energy on the double bond of oxygen, and the lower harmful ultraviolet light rays use up their energy on the single bond of ozone. Who designed our atmosphere to have just the right elements so that we are protected from the harmful light rays, while at the same time so that we get to enjoy the warmth and plant growth and light and beauty of the sun? It sounds like someone who loves us designed something really good.

How about the different types of trees and the different types of food that come out of the ground? What about the different types of animals: some for food and some for beauty? Some are predators, and some are prey, all in a balanced ecosystem. The birds all around, singing joyfully every morning. Domestic animals like dogs and cats, bringing comfort, friendship, and love. And who created love? That's not something that randomly showed up one day, and then the most loving survived!

Just think about these high-level concepts: Where did they come from, and who designed them?

Another thing I looked at was the Bible. I hypothesized that if the Bible was actually words from the living God, I would find amazing things inside. Not just coincidence stuff—I mean *amazing*! So, I searched for them and found quite a few amazing things. Here are some:

Did you know there are over 300 prophecies in the Bible written about Jesus that He fulfilled by His life, death, and resurrection?

- That He would be born of a virgin (Isaiah 7:14).
- He would be born in Bethlehem (Micah 5:2).
- As a child born, He would be God and be from the line of David (Isaiah 9:6).

- He would enter Jerusalem in triumph, riding on a donkey's colt (Zechariah 9:9).

- He would be rejected by His own people (Isaiah 53:1).

- His close friend would betray Him (Psalm 41:9 and Psalm 55:12).

- He would be betrayed for thirty pieces of silver (Zechariah 11:12).

- He would be tried and condemned to death, but the people would not realize He was dying for their sins (Isaiah 53:8).

- He would be silent before His accusers (Isaiah 53:7).

- He would be mocked and taunted (Psalm 22:7).

- He would die by crucifixion, which hadn't yet been invented when the Scriptures were written (Psalm 22:14 and Zechariah 12:10).

- He would be lumped together with other sinners as He was crucified with two criminals (Isaiah 53:12).

- His garments would be divided by casting lots (Psalm 22:18).

- His bones would not be broken as they normally did to hasten the death of those being crucified (Numbers 9:12).

- He would die as a sin offering (Isaiah 53:5).

- He would be buried in a rich man's tomb. (Isaiah 53:9).

- He would be raised from the dead (Psalm 16:10 and Psalm 30:3).

And on and on. And Jesus fulfilled them; it is nothing short of amazing!

The Christian Broadcasting Network, CBN, puts it this way:

Mathematically speaking, the odds of anyone fulfilling this amount of prophecy are staggering. Mathematicians put it this way:

- 1 person fulfilling 8 prophecies: 1 in 100,000,000,000,000,000

- 1 person fulfilling 48 prophecies: 1 chance in 10 to the 157th power

- 1 person fulfilling 300+ prophecies: Only Jesus![1]

---

[1] "Biblical Prophecies Fulfilled by Jesus," CBN.com, accessed November 26, 2021, https://www1.cbn.com/biblestudy/biblical-prophecies-fulfilled-by-jesus.

That's just incredible! But as you might expect from a huge God, there's more. The book of Daniel describes the world powers that would rule, in order, after Daniel's time: the Babylonians, the Medo-Persians, the Greeks, and the Roman Empire, with no other world power after that. And, of course, that's exactly how history unfolded. Only God can announce in advance what He will do and then do it. In great detail too! After Alexander the Great quickly conquers the entire known world, the Bible goes into detail that when he dies, his four generals each take over a section of the empire. Then it goes into soap-opera-level detail about the king of the north trying to trick the king of the south with his daughter Cleopatra. And that's exactly how it went!

One of the best resources I've found that compares the book of Daniel against history is Beth Moore's ladies' Bible study on Daniel. When I heard my wife listening to that study, I couldn't stop myself from tuning in. I found it to be so thorough and well done that we did that study in our Bible study and in two of our small groups!

The book of Ezekiel, chapter 37, talks about the dry bones of Israel coming to life. And in Isaiah 66:8, God declares, "Can a country be born in a day or a nation be brought forth in a moment? Yet no sooner is Zion in labor than she gives birth to her children." And in 1948, after pictures of the pile of bones from the six million Jews brutally killed in the Holocaust surfaced, the nation of Israel was reestablished in one day on May 14, 1948, just as the Bible said it would.

God also said in Isaiah 11:11–12:

In that day the Lord will reach out his hand a second time to reclaim the surviving remnant of his people from Assyria, from Lower Egypt, from Upper Egypt, from Cush, from Elam, from Babylonia, from Hamath and from the islands of the Mediterranean. He will raise a banner for the nations and gather the exiles of Israel; he will assemble the scattered people of Judah from the four quarters of the earth.

And in the three years following the new Jewish state, 700,000 Jews emigrated to Israel.

Did you know, by the way, that Israel was attacked the day after they became a nation on May 14, 1948? Would you expect a nation that is one day old to survive an attack from multiple surrounding nations? Egypt, Iraq, Syria, Lebanon, Saudi Arabia, and Yemen attacked Israeli forces instead of accepting the UN partition plan for an Arab state and a Jewish state. Why did Israel survive? Well, at the high level, they survived because God said He would bring them back and protect them.

Remember we talked about the world empires coming after Babylon in Daniel's time? Well, the Medo-Persians were next on God's timeline. So, after the fall of Babylon to the Medo-Persian king Cyrus the Great in 539 BC, he allowed the Jewish people exiled in Babylon to return to Judah and rebuild the temple for God in Jerusalem. Nearly 50,000 Jews traveled from Babylon to Jerusalem. This was written about by Isaiah 150 years beforehand in Isaiah 44:24–28:

> *This is what the Lord says—your Redeemer, who formed you in the womb: I am the Lord, the Maker of all things, who stretches out the heavens, who spreads out the earth by myself [...] who says to the watery deep, "Be dry, and I will dry up your streams," who says of Cyrus, "He is my shepherd and will accomplish all that I please; he will say of Jerusalem, 'Let it be rebuilt,' and of the temple, 'Let its foundations be laid.'"*

And that's exactly what took place 150 years later!

This amazing prophecy is recorded before Jerusalem is even seized by Nebuchadnezzar, king of Babylon. God predicts the restoration of Jerusalem before it is destroyed. And He records Cyrus's name as the one He will use! The first-century non-Christian historian Josephus (*Antiquities of the Jews*, book 11) says that Isaiah 44 was shown to King Cyrus soon after he conquered Babylon. Can you imagine what King Cyrus thought when he found out a Jewish prophecy named him, talked about his conquering of Babylon, and talked about his plan to send them back as free people to rebuild their temple and their land? How cool is God?

There's even more about Cyrus, talking about redirecting the waters of the Euphrates in verse 27. It turns out that's how Cyrus's general got inside Babylon. He redirected the Euphrates river in another direction, and the Euphrates, which went under the wall to give water to Babylon, dried up, so the army could go in under the wall. And by the way, history records they found the gates under the wall were not locked, and Isaiah 45:1–5 says,

> *This is what the Lord says to his anointed, to Cyrus, whose right hand I take hold of to subdue nations before him and to strip kings of their armor, to open doors before him so that gates will not be shut [...] I am the Lord, and there is no other; apart from me there is no God.*

There's so much more too! I'm telling you: you can't read this stuff and not say, "Oh my God, my God, You have revealed Yourself to all of us!"

And does the Bible answer all those questions you have? You bet it does. One main question I had was why do I still sometimes act in a selfish way, and why do I still have unholy thoughts? Then I read Galatians 5:17: "For the flesh desires what is contrary to the Spirit, and the Spirit what is contrary to the flesh. They are in conflict with each other, so that you are not to do whatever you want."

Paul is talking to believers in Christ, and he's explaining why there is a battle that takes place within every believer. So, when a person who was a jerk surrenders to the Lord Jesus and receives forgiveness of sins and has the Spirit of the living God inside of them instantly, they don't become Jesus. They just become a saved jerk!

Doesn't that explain why you've been hurt at church? Doesn't that explain why you've seen Christians do dumb or even hurtful things? We don't become perfect in every way on day one, but step by step, as we read the Word of God and understand it and learn the things of God, we improve and become more and more like Jesus, inch by inch. Romans 12:2 says:

> *Do not conform to the pattern of this world, but be transformed by the renewing of your mind. Then you will be able to test and approve what God's will is—his good, pleasing and perfect will.*

Do you see how, step by step, we change our minds as we read what God says and realize what God's will is for a given topic? We might recognize our selfishness and focus on God and others instead of ourselves 99.9 percent of the time. I've been working on that for years, and I think I've reduced my selfish thoughts all the way down to 95 percent of the time now!

But will you read the Word of God? Will you allow your mind to be transformed by God? Will you measure it against history? Do you even know history? Why isn't this detail about history being taught in schools any longer? Don't get me started on public schools; we quickly realized we needed to homeschool our three children, and that was long before the current levels of indoctrination and agendas!

There's something so fantastic about proving the Bible is the inerrant (without error) living word of God, too: we don't have to trust a human to understand God. We have an objective book we can turn to for understanding God, rather than trusting a pastor or a priest or someone's opinion who might have an agenda. We can read it for ourselves and make our own decisions. That is wonderfully freeing, isn't it?

There's more evidence that I found at the high level. If Jesus was really God on the earth, did He say anything godlike? Of course, He did! In Matthew 16:18, Jesus said, "And I tell you that you are Peter, and on this rock, I will build my church, and the gates of Hades will not overcome it." Jesus said this in response to Peter declaring that Jesus is the Christ. And upon that revelation, Jesus said He was building His church and nothing would stand against it. Not even the gates of hell.

Well, Jesus and His followers, His church, were basically a startup religion in Israel at that time. These Christians were claiming their Jewish neighbors just killed the Messiah that they had been waiting for, so they were hated by their Jewish community. They were also a startup religion in an area that was controlled and oppressed by the powerful Roman Empire. The Romans barely tolerated the Jews but gave them some leeway because they had been doing the same things for thousands of years. But this new startup religion was met with brutal force when they did not bow to Caesar, stating they could only bow to the Lord Jesus. They dipped Christians in tar and lit them on fire as human streetlights!

Who expected that the tiny startup religion would still be here today with over two billion people claiming to be part of it and that the powerful Roman Empire would be gone? But Jesus said, "You won't stop My church," and no one did, and no one ever will!

Jesus's high-level summary is also very telling. He said the summary of all the law and all the prophets is this: love God with all your heart and love your neighbor like he's you. Who can argue with that? God wants us to love everyone. God loves everyone. Everyone has high value to Him because He created them, and He doesn't make mistakes. As is, everyone is valuable! Talk about inclusion: He includes everyone! And everyone is invited to accept what He's done to save us. No one is good enough; no one can reach God. Every false religion tries to reach God by doing something, *but God* (those two words again) reached us! It is all from a gift that He delivers. He is just, so His punishment for sin was required, but He is also merciful to us because He poured out the punishment for sin on His Son for our sake. The Creator of life shows us His plans for life lead to love and joy and songs in the home.

Now, the most important high-level piece of evidence I looked at was this: Did the dead guy get up? I mean, that's the whole ball of wax, isn't it? Well, the evidence for the dead guy getting up is great.

I was called to jury duty one day a few years ago and selected to be on the jury for a murder trial. It was a horrible view of why everyone needs a savior, but that's not my point. The prosecution said something I don't think I'll ever forget. She said, "You won't hear the judge tell you that circumstantial evidence is any less important than eyewitness evidence. The reason is because it is not less important." She went on to give an example of how circumstantial evidence can be solid evidence of what happened. Her example was this: if you heard the weatherman say it was expected to snow in the night, you would feel how cold it was, and then you would wake up in the morning and see snow on the ground. That's circumstantial evidence that the snow is on the ground because it snowed. You didn't witness the snow. I could have been on your roof with a snow machine, but it is obvious from the circumstances that it snowed.

Well, the apostles around Jesus were scared to death, ran away, hid, and were depressed, mourning the death of Jesus. But after three days, many people claimed to see Jesus alive again. The apostles now preached Jesus being alive, even when threatened, beaten, flogged, imprisoned, stoned to their last dying breath, and killed in other ways. They never changed their story! Why? Because they saw Him alive. That's obvious!

Chuck Colson, who was lead counsel for the Nixon administration during Watergate, said it this way in his book *Loving God*. He said we were the seven most powerful people in the United States, and arguably, the world. Yet when we were threatened with white-collar prison, we all started changing our stories and telling the truth to protect ourselves and stay out of jail. But these apostles were the weakest people on the planet. They were mostly fishermen with no connections, no influence, no money, no authority, and no power. Yet, they never changed their stories, even as they were killed for saying so. That's some pretty strong circumstantial evidence that they saw the dead guy get up!

This is just the high-level evidence! If you dig into any level of detail in any of these categories, you'll find even more evidence. Like, how about archeology? Did you know that most of the time, archeology matches the biblical record so well that many archeologists start with the Bible? Excavation of the walls of Jericho, located in the southern Jordan valley in Israel, found the walls of Jericho fell outward on all sides except the north side where the prostitute Rahab must have lived.[2]

What about biology? Michael J. Behe, a professor of biochemistry at Lehigh University in Pennsylvania and a senior fellow of the Discovery Institute's Center for Science and Culture, wrote the book *Darwin's Black Box*, where he coins the term "irreducible complexity." In it, he shows that complex biochemical systems within the human body are marvelously designed and could not have evolved. Stephen C. Meyer is a geophysicist and former college professor with a PhD in the philosophy of science from the University of Cambridge. He has some major scientific evidence-based books, like the *New York Times*

---

[2] "Is the Bible accurate concerning the existence and destruction of the walls of Jericho?" ChristianAnswers, accessed November 26, 2021, https://christiananswers. net/q-abr/abr-a011.html.

bestseller called *Darwin's Doubt: The Explosive Origin of Animal Life and the Case for Intelligent Design*. His books are, of course, not just a small step deeper into the details but much deeper, and you'll still find it's true! And there are many, many others.

So, after careful investigation, I found what I needed: the Bible is the full story and the evidence for Christ is overwhelmingly convincing! That's just the written part of what I found.

Remember that this God is whispering stuff to me at the same time. And I really want to hear His whisper, so I'm listening intently. Carefully. There's a spiritual side to all of this; there's more than just what we can see with our eyes. And in my spirit, God is communicating with me.

And He also orchestrates events, people, places, and things! Who can deny all this?

I had already started reading the Bible and, in fact, couldn't put it down. At the same time, I started going to Bible studies and listening to great Bible teachers on Moody Radio, people who knew the Bible and could teach it. That began to open up a world of incredible wonder. I wanted to know who is this God who reached down to save me.

And God responded to me with miracle after miracle after miracle. I'll continue to mention some of them here to encourage you even more.

In 1995, I took a job with Rockwell Semiconductor Systems for a better match of my engineering plus communication skills and for higher pay (let's be honest). In February of 1999, while I was working for Rockwell Semiconductor Systems, which just spun off as Conexant Systems in January that year, a person was hired in the office as an administrator, but I knew she would be a guide to help me go deeper with my understanding and interaction with God. I just knew it ahead of time. I'm not sure how to explain it any more than that; I just knew she would know about God and point me to Him.

Miracle 4. God tells me in advance Donna would be a guide to point me to Him.

At that time, my wife was pregnant with our third child. As his birth approached and we discussed what his name might be, we decided we would pray and have God pick the name. Now, I felt like God said to me that I should let Beckie hear the name from God. So, when the baby was born, we prayed in the delivery room again, and I asked her what she heard from heaven. "Elijah David," she said. And I thought, *Wow, that's pretty biblical sounding, maybe a bit too much!* So I prayed (I can't remember if I prayed out loud or to myself), "Lord, if this is really the name you want, please confirm it in this Bible I see sitting on the shelf!" I felt this faithful confidence that God was driving this, but I shuddered a bit as I pulled the Bible out and noticed it was strictly a New Testament. But I popped it open, and right on that page was Jesus talking about Elijah! That was amazing, and so our third child got his name that day.

Miracle 5. Elijah's name given to us is confirmed miraculously.

Later that month, in July, God said our rental real-estate transaction would not go through, and the buyer backed out five months later, even though she had deposits and payments she would lose.

I have these things in my notes because I was keeping a written journal of things God was saying to me. People don't just walk away from deposits they put down on houses, but in this case, they did!

Miracle 6. God tells us what is to come regarding our rental real-estate transaction five months in advance.

Also, at the house that year, the new tenant's family was struggling (a lot) and needed help. Her boyfriend molested her granddaughters. (This is where people can end up without Jesus: Who would touch a child inappropriately? That's disgusting, but people can end up very far down evil roads without Jesus.) I felt led to pray for her, pray for the girls, pray for the family, and gently explain the gospel to her. And she received Jesus as her Lord and got saved. Her son (the father of the girls) also accepted Jesus in jail! He was then released from prison (suddenly, I think) to be with his girls, and his wife (mother of the girls) started cleaning up her life by getting help.

Miracles 7, 8, and *9.* God's grace reaches the grandmother, the father, the mother, and the girls, and who knows how many miracles continued from there in their life, now that they have Jesus.

In December of that same year (1999 still), after the Christmas play, the Lord gave me a vision of a bunch of believers on the Pinellas Trail, holding hands and praising the Lord. I told Pastor Herb Lange about it, and he said, "It will happen!" with total confidence. So, I believed it.

Seventeen months or so later, in May 2001, for the National Day of Prayer, Somebody Cares Tampa Bay, with Dr. Daniel Bernard leading, held a Day of Prayer on the Pinellas Trail.

Miracle 10. God gives me a vision seventeen months ahead of time for the gathering He would orchestrate on the Pinellas Trail and gives confidence to Pastor Lange that it is Him.

In June of 2000, while a bit sick, lying in bed, I received words from God to write down. It's a bit of a summary of the good news of Jesus and a wake-up call. More on this in a bit. I'm doing this somewhat chronologically, so you can see some timeline of God's revelations and blessings.

In March of 2001, God had me call a woman I met at the Juvenile Justice meetings. Her name is Ella, and I had her card in my wallet for a long time (two years maybe?). So, I pulled the car over to the curb immediately, and I called her at God's prompting, and she said she needed encouraging at just that time. She was just praying!

Miracle 11. God answers Ella's prayer for His encouragement by telling me to call her.

Now let me stop right there: maybe you're thinking these are not miracles, these are just answered prayers. Okay, whatever you call them—revelations, miracles, answered prayers—these are documented real interactions with the living, risen, Lord Jesus Christ, and wait until you see what He did next!

And I mean documented because I still have many of my notes from over twenty years ago right here in front of me. Yes, I really do! The

Lord wouldn't let me throw them out (much to my wife's chagrin: she's not a saver; she's a thrower.)

Miracle 12. God tells me over twenty years in advance to save my notes for a book He will want me to write. I'm talking about this book; in case you're not paying much attention here, do you need another cup of coffee? Well, you might want to get one before I tell you this next one.

Also in March 2001, I attended one of the best Bible studies I did, called Experiencing God, by Henry Blackaby. It was awesome! God did such an amazing thing during that Bible study; He basically spoon-fed me, little by little. Sometimes, as I learned what was possible from the Bible and this Bible study, God would do it. It was amazing! And this Bible study was led by two awesome people of God, Larry and Sue Kuhlman. They were so authentic and so calm and patient, so joyful and full of faith, that the "baby inside would jump" (read Luke 1:44 if you don't get that) during that Bible study. They helped many people understand the beautiful news of Christ.

On September 6, 2001, Ella Mae Warren calls me and asks if she can interview me regarding what God is saying to me. She does a radio show, and she feels God wants her to talk to me. I tell her I don't have anything to say, but if God really wants it, I'll do my best.

September 9, at church, I feel a strong pull to cry out for the people of Sudan. God gives me a vision of two big dudes in tuxedos lifting me up, and it makes me stand up. I walk up to Pastor Lange timidly and tell him I think God wants him to pray for Sudan (I don't even know where Sudan is really, without having a Google map open!). Herb says, "Go ahead; you pray," and hands me the microphone. I tremble; I don't even know if I'm hearing anything correctly. I don't know how this invisible communication works: What if I'm not hearing the words right? It's one thing for me to make a phone call or drive out of my way (more on that later) but talk to the whole congregation? Pray with them? I stumble through a prayer for Christians being persecuted in Sudan, give him back the mic, and go sit down.

As we drive home from church that morning, I wonder if I was supposed to do that or if I have just made a fool of myself. I wonder if I can really hear God at all. And just like that, I hear Him say (rather abruptly), "Go anyway." So, I say it out loud, "Go anyway." And Beckie (my wife, if you haven't been paying attention) says, "Go where?" And I say, "I don't know." Then God tells me, "To Ella's radio show!" And so I say, "To Ella's radio show! I haven't heard from her even though today's the afternoon I'm supposed to meet with her." Beckie says, "Well, you go; I'm sitting down with a magazine today."

So, I go to the WTAN radio station, and Chip Collins is there; he's running things, and as we approach the time of her show and Ella is still not around, Chip seems a bit frantic, like he's scrambling to get music lined up. God says to me, "Read the note," and I pray back, "What note?" and He says, "When you were sick [back in June]." Oh! That note! So, I say to Chip, "Hey, Chip, I know what I'm supposed to say," and Chip says, "Then sit down right there [because we were on in sixty seconds]." So, I sit down and put some headsets on in front of a microphone. He pushes a few buttons, says something, and then points to me.

God takes over; I just read what was written on the paper three months in advance. A wake-up call to whoever is listening, "People, Jesus came in the flesh and lived a sinless life so he could pay the penalty for our sins that we can't pay. He paid it in full, and anyone, anyone, can be forgiven if they just believe in Him, turn from their sins, and surrender to His leadership, His Lordship; because out of love, He took care of everything that separates us from being with our heavenly Father who loves us. Turn to Him!"

It was a bit longer than that, but you get the gist of it. The instant I'm done with what is written on the paper, the twenty-nine-minute time is up, and Chip pushes a button for some music, and I'm done.

Miracle 13. God gives me words to speak in advance.

Miracle 14. God tells Ella to invite me.

Miracle 15. God tells me to go anyway, even though Ella did not call nor confirm (it turns out she had car trouble with no cell signal).

Miracle 16. Chip is ready and okay for me to sit down and read what I have. God orchestrates the radio show to give a wake-up call.

And you know what happened two days later, on September 11, 2001,—the terrible terror attack on the United States twin towers in New York City (and the Pentagon and others)!

Miracle 17. Only God knows who heard what was read that day in advance of a coming tragedy. In His mercy and grace, He reaches out to certain people through me; don't ask me why—I'm just an imperfect human like everyone else, but I have this Spirit of the sovereign Lord inside me, and He can do amazing things. I can't do anything useful without Him, but He can do anything in the name of Jesus, the Creator and Leader of the universe. And He can do lots more through you too! Jesus made that clear in John 14:8–21; read as Philip talks to Jesus (I added the italics hereinafter, in case you didn't know):

Philip said, "Lord, show us the Father and that will be enough for us."

Jesus answered: "Don't you know me, Philip, even after I have been among you such a long time? Anyone who has seen me has seen the Father. How can you say, 'Show us the Father'? Don't you believe that I am in the Father, and that the Father is in me? The words I say to you I do not speak on my own authority. Rather, it is the Father, living in me, who is doing his work. Believe me when I say that I am in the Father and the Father is in me; or at least believe on the evidence of the works themselves. Very truly I tell you, *whoever believes in me will do the works I have been doing, and they will do even greater things than these*, because I am going to the Father. And I will do whatever you ask in my name, so that the Father may be glorified in the Son. You may ask me for anything in my name, and I will do it.

"If you love me, keep my commands. And I will ask the Father, and he will give you another advocate to help you and be with you forever—the Spirit of truth. The world cannot accept him, because it neither sees him nor knows him. But you know him, *for he lives with you and will be in you.* I will not leave you as orphans; I will come to you. Before long, the world will not see me anymore, but you will see me. Because I live, you also will live. On that day you will realize that I am in my Father, and you are in me, and I am in you. Whoever has my commands and keeps them is the one who loves me. The one who loves me will be loved by my Father, and I too will love them and show myself to them."

—JOHN 14:8–21

There it is: the Spirit of truth (the Holy Spirit, the third part of God) lives in believers, and we will do the works Jesus has been doing (and greater). What? He trusts us with that?

ROOTS

One of the things I read in the Bible was that Jesus said, "My sheep hear my voice" (John 10:27, KJV) and also that the Holy Spirit leads us. One night, I felt God pointing me to something, leading me into the parking lot of our church, and having me take notice of a big tree. I could've easily ignored the "tap on the shoulder," as I like to call it, but I didn't. Also, I didn't see any harm in looking at a tree, so I paused to drink in whatever God might be saying, pointing to. Then I felt the Spirit of God leading me directly across the street to another church, which also had a big tree. Our church was a UMC church, First United Methodist Church of Tarpon Springs, and across the street was the Assembly of God church. There was something I was supposed to notice; I could just tell. I noticed they had a Bible study that met there, just like our church, and various other similar events, just like ours.

I felt like God wanted to say more, and I tried to stay focused on Him. So, I went home and told Beckie that God was saying something and that I needed to go into a room and pray. She said, "Okay." When I went to the bedroom by myself and prayed, I could see both trees and then more trees. And I felt Him say to me, "See all the trees: they all come to Me." At that point, I could see all the roots of all these trees were joined together way down into the earth. I felt like He was saying, "All the churches are Mine, so they all should be united and coming to Me." Later I would find this obvious biblical concept: Jesus is the head of the body of Christ, which is the church. All the churches should have one leader, Jesus!

This, of course, spurred questions about denominations and, ultimately, church history. How did we get to so many denominations? What's the difference? Why can't I find denominations in the Bible? Some of this is answered, I learned, by different callings that different churches have, but some of it is also from people trying to create their own subkingdoms. But I learned, Jesus prays, in fact, in John 17, that we, all the believers and followers of Jesus, would be *one*, or united.

Miracle 18. God reveals His continued call to unity through a vision. This unity concept would come up again and again for me.

I happened to be up to Romans 11, and God says through Paul in verse 17 that the Jews and Gentiles are all part of the same body of believers (unity), and Paul uses roots of an olive tree to make his point too:

> *If some of the branches have been broken off, and you, though a wild olive shoot, have been grafted in among the others and now share in the nourishing sap from the olive root, do not consider yourself to be superior to those other branches. If you do, consider this: You do not support the root, but the root supports you.*
>
> —*Romans 11:17–18*

Miracle 19. God confirms His unity revelation through my daily Bible reading.

Also in 2001, at one point, I felt like the Holy Spirit was leading me to cash in my stock options and pay off the mortgage on the house. We didn't pray about it further, and we didn't do it, and boy, did we regret that later! Our company's stock dropped like a rock, and we missed a good opportunity. After that, of course, I decided to try hard to listen to what God was whispering.

Moving forward to 2002: as I started to tell you, I was working for a semiconductor company, and I was laid off in the economic downturn. It sure would have been great to have the house paid off then. As my wife and I prayed about what God wanted us to do, I felt Him lead us to something insane. I mean *really* insane!

God gave me this crazy vision to start a company. I remember praying for Him to confirm it because it would be total financial suicide if it were not from God! It would be like stepping off a financial cliff. Then, I remembered, *Oh my God, I wrote that down in my journal!*

A youth minister (Neil) left our church in Tarpon and felt led to take a ministry position at a small church that couldn't afford to pay him.

I asked him, "Neil, how are you and your wife doing [with two small children, one in diapers]?" He said, "Rich, you can't tell that the hand of God can hold you up when He calls you to step off a cliff until you step off the cliff!" And as he said it, something beamed straight to my heart. I knew something was up with that so much that I wrote it down in my prayer journal.

Miracle 20. God had me write "stepping off a cliff" ahead of time! And eighteen months later, there we were being called to step off a cliff.

I thought, *Really, God? Wow! You had me write that down eighteen months in advance so I would know that it's You!* I was excited and scared to death at the same time.

Beckie and I prayed and fasted and prayed and prayed. Our prayer was, "God, if it's Your will to start a company, please confirm it, make it clear, and open the door." We prayed that a lot!

One day, my wife said, "We prayed that prayer already, and so God's answered it. Let's ask God to move it forward now!"

GO EARLY

There's no way to explain where we are right now in 2021, except that God is big, He loves us, and no one can stop His plans, no one!

Everyone knows how crazy the COVID-19 pandemic was in 2020 and 2021, but what you may not know is many, many people experienced God in profound ways. We did!

We normally fly to Florida, where we kept our home and rented it as a short-term rental, but in about July of 2020, both my wife and I, separately, felt like God said, "Go to Florida early. Drive." And I try hard to pay attention if we both get the same thing from heaven separately for obvious reasons: the chances of us hearing it correctly are increased. You may recall that the Bible says we see through a glass, dimly lit, in 1 Corinthians 13:12. So, I always want to get my nose all the way up to the glass, wipe away the condensation, and look (listen) carefully. My problem is I always want to but don't always do it.

We prayed together and decided it was from God and we should take two weeks' vacation by driving to Florida in September instead of December. Well, we weren't on the road five days before we got word that my ninety-four-year-old mother fell, perhaps confirming one of the reasons the Holy Spirit whispered, "Go early."

Miracle 21. God says, "Go early to Florida," for us to be there for my mom and other things coming.

Between mid-September and November, my mother fell two more times, sending her to the ER with stitches, and we were able to move her to my aunt's house.

On November 11, during a reroof, our house in Florida flooded because the roofing company didn't tarp the house after removing the old roof, with the tropical storm Eta approaching! It rained inside the house. The amazing thing that night was that even though the water was coming out of air-conditioner vents and ceiling fans, basically raining in the house, it did not rain on us. We were still able to sleep there—thank you, Lord!

Miracle 22. Though most of the roof is exposed, and it's raining in our house, it is not raining in Rebecca's (our special-needs daughter) room, nor our son's room, nor one other room where my wife and I dragged our mattress to get some sleep.

That water damage forced us to leave our home with our special-needs daughter, who normally doesn't cope well with change, and go to rental houses. Partly because of the incompetence of the first repair company, who could not give us a repair schedule, and partly because it was winter in Florida, so rentals were hard to find available, we had to move seven times. *But God* is faithful!

Miracle 23. Though we moved seven times, our daughter did not totally melt down. God intervened (and always will)!

We have a house on the water in Florida, so we asked for at least the same accommodations, and God came through beautifully: wonderful houses to rent on the water (in Florida, during the busy winter season!). One of the houses we rented was in a large waterfront community. The houses were all well-kept, the people very friendly, and the neighborhood was just so inviting that my wife said, "Honey, I want to live here! Let's sell the other house and buy something in here." Since we had already moved six times to rental houses, another house would also allow us to stop moving since there was still no end in sight to the repairs. And we really needed to end the moving. So, we prayed about that and felt like God was revealing the wisdom in selling our house now, during a seller's market, after it gets rebuilt. We were almost being forced to sell because we couldn't rent it during this entire time, but we were still paying all the bills. We turned away tons of people who wanted to rent our house. But the rebuilding would be like a remodeling if we poured more effort, money, and planning into it!

Miracle 24. God turns our house water damage into good. Romans 8:28 says: "And we know that in all things God works for the good of those who love him, who have been called according to his purpose."

I told you about the view from the rental: looking out across the flat water, we could see a boat three miles offshore, just sitting there for weeks. The view of the Gulf of Mexico in this area of Florida is one of my favorite views on earth, and God knew we needed that flat, still water.

God is the source of our strength and peace, and somehow He gets us through things, amazing things where there is no way, such as ten years of not earning money for the house, three and a half years of absolute zero income for the house from the fruits of our labor; yet somehow every bill got paid, nothing was lost, and we even thrived! More on those soon, but back to the houses: we started looking for a home to buy in that community, but all of them were selling at super high prices and very quickly. I'm sure you've heard that with all the COVID-19 craziness, the work-from-home craze, and the stock-market uncertainty, real estate is selling quickly and at super high prices right now.

We became frustrated and tired after a few weeks of looking. Then, I'm embarrassed to say, we decided to pray for God to point us to the house He had in mind. You would think by now I would remember to pray first! No sense in wasting our time with other things. We were tired of looking, tired of taking care of the house repairs, and tired of many other things. In fact, my wife prayed that God would just bring us the house and that we would just wait on Him. And so God did!

Our friends popped up out of nowhere and said their mother was considering selling her house, and if we wanted to buy it, we could do so with no real estate agent and save some money! God is good. (All the time! That's the response of ten thousand men I heard in the Tampa Ice Palace during Promise Keepers, a glorious sound.)

Miracle 25. God brings us the house to buy at a good price in a seller's market.

That's the same thing He did in Oregon, by the way. That's coming up later.

After moving six times, with a special-needs daughter who normally doesn't cope well with change, we could now move one last time and then stop moving while the repairs on our old house took place. By God's grace, we made it through those other moves. Just to put that in perspective: the one move to Oregon in 2014 landed us in the ER, and this was *seven* moves. *But God* had different plans! Chuck Swindoll, founder of Insight for Living Ministry, senior pastor of Stonebriar Community Church in Frisco, Texas, and former president of Dallas Theological Seminary, says that's the Gospel in two words, "but God!"

Chuck Swindoll is one of those great Bible teachers on Moody Radio that I listened to early on. He's fantastic and has a way of putting things from the Scriptures so clearly.

During the same period from September 2020 through April 2021, when we came to Florida early, the Lord also helped me continue and complete a huge deal at Intel, where I worked. This deal was an immense potential customer that many did not think would come to fruition, and it took many hours, dealing with many, many partners (everyone wanted to win this business) and many different groups within Intel over the course of about eighteen months. When the technical support specialist and I closed the deal at the end of 2020, in December, it was triple our target! We achieved 300 percent of our target, but somehow in April 2021, my time at Intel was done. Never mind the details: when God opens a door, no man can shut it (Revelation 3:8), and when God closes a door, no man can open it.

God did wonderful things at Intel and blessed others and me while I was there. The Intel Bible-based Christian Network (IBCN) has been making great strides in the past few years. When I arrived in 2014 in Hillsboro, Oregon (God moved us 3,500 miles across the country. I didn't even know where Hillsboro was!), I found out Intel had a Christian group. There was a local Bible study group on the floor where I was working, so I joined them. After a short time, they needed a leader to take over the weekly Bible study group—I told you God tends to do that with me. I extended the Bible study to include dial-in from any remote location for other salespeople.

Eventually, our global IBCN lead, Theo, approached me and asked if I would pray about leading a virtual group to reach the hundreds of people who are part of the Intel IBCN group but don't live near an

Intel large campus. Not just remote salespeople but anyone remote. After prayer, I said yes, and this became the virtual group that anyone could join. Of course, for some, the time zone would be difficult, but we decided to do our best to make it available.

During the COVID-19 pandemic, over one hundred people tuned into this Bible study for an hour of devotion, Scripture, prayer, discussion, and encouragement.

Miracle 26. God uses the small weekly Bible study to encourage many employees for over a year (and still going) during the crazy pandemic times.

Next, the Lord put on the heart of our new IBCN global lead, Craig Carter, to add to the IBCN global leadership structure. Beyond geographic leadership, he felt led to add a strategic leader in four areas. One of those areas he called the "Grow" team, whose charter is to grow IBCN by reaching out to international Intel locations to help them know they are part of a larger family, help them get through any HR hurdles, and most importantly, love them and pray with them and for them, and join arm in arm with them as brothers and sisters in Christ.

Craig asked me to colead this group, and before we even put structure to this new group, the Lord brought a bunch of leaders in nations that we wanted to reach. Someone from Thailand had a Bible study group and wanted to be on the Grow team and to be the leader for Thailand. The same happened with Malaysia, Germany, and others. We called one person in Israel, out of four that we had on the IBCN list, and asked him if he wanted to be the lead for Intel IBCN Israel, and he said yes. It was that simple! God had already prepared everything in advance. Our hearts burst with joy and gratitude!

Miracle 27. God prepares the hearts and minds of different people to be ready to join the leadership roles for the Intel Christian group in many global locations.

It was as if I was told to walk along the beach and help the turtles by pointing them back to the ocean where they belonged. There are so many turtles, and as I walk, turtles just show up, and while I point some of them back to the ocean, other turtle helpers see me, and I see them. We thought we were the only turtle workers on the beach, but we're not. So, we encourage each other to just keep walking along the beach mapped out for us!

Hebrews 12:1–3 says:

> *Let us run with perseverance the race marked out for us, fixing our eyes on Jesus, the pioneer and perfecter of faith. For the joy set before him he endured the cross, scorning its shame, and sat down at the right hand of the throne of God. Consider him who endured such opposition from sinners, so that you will not grow weary and lose heart.*

The next thing we knew, there were now dozens of us on the beach, making a much bigger impact on the turtle population!

I hope you like analogies because that's my go-to technique for making a point. God seems to give me analogies (or maybe I watched too much TV in the '70s).

What is also awesome is that for the last three years, I have been feeling strongly led to always have a coleader or two serve with me, as I sensed that at any moment, things could change and God would call me away. So, the Tuesday noon Bible study had two other coleaders, the Grow team had a coleader, and the previous service I did for Easter events and Christmas events had other coleaders. As a result, when I suddenly left, nothing even skipped a beat! Instead, God could now send my wife, our daughter, and me elsewhere to minister to other people and be ministered to because, let me tell you, we need that too!

Miracle 28. God has me prepare coleaders at Intel in advance, and then three years later, I have a sudden departure from Intel.

So here I sit, in Florida for the last eight months, in a new house, getting repairs on the old house, and letting the Lord work all things together for our good, including my ninety-four-year-old mother's needs, my special-needs daughter's needs, my wife's needs, my needs, our insurance-claim needs, and on and on.

God is so good that the pastor of the church we're attending is preaching on how to enter God's rest in spite of the chaos around us. Do you know this rest that is mentioned in Hebrews 4? It reads as follows, starting with verse 6:

> *Therefore, since it still remains for some to enter that rest, and since those who formerly had the good news proclaimed to them did not go in because of their disobedience, God again set a certain day, calling it "Today." This he did when a long time later he spoke through David, as in the passage already quoted: "Today, if you hear his voice, do not harden your hearts." For if Joshua had given them rest, God would not have spoken later about another day.*
>
> —*HEBREWS 4:6–8*

There remains, then, a Sabbath rest for the people of God. That's good news! We have available to us, as believers, a rest that is independent of circumstances. This rest, Pastor Aaron Derksen of West Coast Word of Faith Church in Tarpon Springs, Florida, preached, does not require inactivity, and it is also not laziness. We can be (and should be) at rest while working hard or while taking a break. It is a spiritual rest, entered into by faith.

Man, at just the right time, God brings a message to me through Pastor Aaron: "Rich, you can't do this by human effort! There's no sense in stressing and striving so hard. I know the list is long, but you're covered. He's got this! Instead, enter into God's Sabbath rest.

"Ah, still waters…lush green grass…Can you see them? Can you smell the aroma of the water and the grass? Can you rest in Him, Rich? Can you let go again, Rich? Today again?

"I know you let go two days ago, but you're stressing again. Can you stir your faith up to trust Him again, Rich? To rest in the shadow of His massive, powerful wings? Protected, comforted, loved—as is! Just come back to the secret hiding shelter of the Most High and rest!"

Miracle 29. God brings the right "Rest" message at just the right time. (He's done this hundreds and hundreds of times, so this really should be miracle number 629!)

So, while I'm resting, "I will do more through you," the Spirit of God whispers to me, "but you can still rest in Me the whole time. Every day."

Then, from the blind side, *bam*! We're fighting (verbally)—my wife and I—with each other, not in agreement, tired from the chaos, tired from battling with contractors, insurance people, documentation, our daughter is acting out from her own frustrations (that she can't name or communicate to us very well, but she's getting better at it by God's grace), tired of doctors' visits for my mother. Mom can't stay where she is, but we think we are only here temporarily and already burning out; it's just sudden! We're fighting, screaming, cursing. (Sorry, but that's the real story; too much honesty for you?)

But God (there's the Gospel again in two words) has people praying for us: my Intel brothers and sisters and our small groups, which include one in Oregon and one in Florida. Our Florida small group of believer friends are scheduled to come over Friday. To continue my honesty: a part of me wants to cancel and just focus on the problems at hand, but that's the opposite of what God says to do. God says through King David in Psalm 34,

> *O magnify the Lord with me, and let us exalt his name together. I sought the Lord, and he heard me, and delivered me from all my fears. They looked unto Him, and were lightened: and their faces were not ashamed.*
>
> *This poor man cried, and the Lord heard him, and saved him out of all his troubles. The angel of the Lord encampeth round about them that fear him, and delivereth them.*
>
> *O taste and see that the Lord is good: blessed is the man that trusteth in him.*
>
> — PSALM 34:3–8 (KJV)

In other words, as Pastor Lesley said when he preached on Sunday, "Magnify the Lord with me. If you take a magnifying glass, the item you are focusing on gets bigger to you but not to anyone else. If you aim the magnifying glass on your problems, if you and your wife talk about the problem before going to bed (or argue about it!), and if you talk about it in the morning and worry about it all through the day, the problem will get enormous to you (but it hasn't changed). But if instead, you focus your magnifying glass on God, you make Him larger, but you can't make Him larger than He really is because nothing is larger than God, nothing! And then, you can worship this God who loves you and let Him save you out of all your troubles. That's what the Word says, so that's what we can rely on, by faith. If God said He'll do it in His Word, He will do it!"

I know what you're thinking, *Rich, you don't know the facts of what I'm facing!* Well, my facts were pretty bad, too; with all the troubles listed above, we had quite a list of facts to face.

But here's what God did: the small group came over, ate with us, chatted with us, and prayed for us and with us Friday night at our house. I explained the problem and the facts of the problem (current focus: the problem facts + current magnification of the problem facts = stress). Nicole reminded us that Abraham also faced the facts. In Romans 4, we're told that Abraham faced the fact that he was one hundred years old, and his wife was old (seventy-five, I think) and therefore barren, and they were childless. Those are the facts. *But* listen to what Abraham did in Romans 4:18–21:

> *Against all hope, Abraham in hope believed and so became the father of many nations, just as it had been said to him, "So shall your offspring be." Without weakening in his faith, he faced the fact that his body was as good as dead—since he was about a hundred years old—and that Sarah's womb was also dead. Yet he did not waver through unbelief regarding the promise of God, but was strengthened in his faith and gave glory to God, being fully persuaded that God had power to do what he had promised.*

Abraham gave glory to God, or said differently, turned the magnifying glass onto God. And, by the way, if you don't know the story, the old guy did indeed have children at one hundred years old. He had Isaac, by faith! Who went on to have Jacob, renamed to Israel, as you may know.

So, I let go again Friday night. "God will solve this," I merely said. I almost cried at the table, thinking of how much God loves my wife and me to send our friends to meet with us, eat with us, pray with us, and then give us this perfect message at just the right time! I almost cried, but I grew up with "real men don't cry," so I didn't. Too much honesty again?

Miracle 30. God has just the right message to encourage us (again) to rest in Him and keep the faith despite the facts, going with joy and peace instead. He's got this covered!

And in amazing but usual God's fashion, the pastor reiterated the same scripture on Sunday; yep, he basically started with Romans 4:18, "Abraham faced the fact but did not waver through unbelief but gave glory to God, being fully persuaded God could do it!" How does God do that? Does He pay that much attention to my details? Yes, He does! The Lord pays attention to every one of our details because of His love for us!

As a result of our faith, by Saturday morning, the "storm" passed, my wife and I had agreement on what to do, and all was calm again. God is so good! He won't let anything through to you that He can't turn into good! Said differently: in all things, God works for the good.

Wow, I heard that! You just thought of that painful thing that has decreased your faith. You wonder, "How can a good God allow suffering like some I went through?" I know some of us have very painful suffering that we have gone through or are in the midst of. Please pray right now and listen with a softened heart to hear from heaven. I am so sorry that you had to go through this pain. But God is always working toward the good of many people, and sometimes we won't understand it all until we get face-to-face with God in heaven. What helps in the meantime is getting alone now, in the presence of God.

This topic is sometimes a barrier to belief for some people. I had a woman ask me some questions about God, and then she brought out that question. She asked, "Why would God take a good man early?" That's a big, important question, and you can hear from that question that she knew a guy who was a good man and that he died early. God, in His Word, gives us one of His reasons in Isaiah 57:1: "The righteous perish, and no one takes it to heart; the devout are taken away, and no one understands that the righteous are taken away to be spared from evil."

God says, "Sometimes I take a good man early to spare him from the evil that was coming." Inherent in that logic is that he went to a better place. You can't be spared from evil if you went to just die. But since Jesus demonstrated power over death by resurrecting, we know this righteous man, because of what Jesus has done, can live even though he died.

Let's take it a step further. How about a child, an innocent child that everyone knows has done nothing wrong but yet dies? Not at the hand of evil, because, in this broken world, we also have evil driven by the devil. But maybe this innocent child died from a disease, and maybe people prayed. Why would God allow that?

This child will obviously miss out on all things in this life. To understand the answer, we have to include not just this life but also eternity. We have to get to heaven and ask the child if God made it up to them since they missed out on sports and friends and marriage and parenting. In heaven, that child will say, "Absolutely, He did!"

You see, the cross proves that this God loves us. This is the real story. This love is so strong and is given without any conditions. This love drove our heavenly Father to send His one Son to die so that we don't have to die. This child, who is in heaven, no longer misses out. The righteous man, who God takes early to save him from evil, didn't miss out but rather is in the best of the best places. And your loved one did not miss out either. The earth's joys and riches and pleasures pale in comparison to heaven's. Being directly with Jesus is the ultimate fulfillment that is inside every person too!

It's hard to comprehend this love that God has for us. Paul said in Ephesians 3:17–19 that it takes power to try and understand it. God says through Paul:

And I pray that you, being rooted and established in love, may have power, together with all the Lord's holy people, to grasp how wide and long and high and deep is the love of Christ, and to know this love that surpasses knowledge—that you may be filled to the measure of all the fullness of God.

— *EPHESIANS 3:17–19*

I picture Paul standing on the beach, looking out across the ocean. How wide and far can the eye see right now? God's love is wider and further! How high does the sky go up, and how deep does the ocean go down? God's love for you goes higher and deeper! Can you grasp that? Try; it takes power to grasp that.

Now, can you know that love? Because when you know that love, you can be filled all the way up. I have to really work to grasp this love and meditate on God to know this love. If I catch a small piece of it, I'm filled with something so satisfying that I no longer think about myself but rather about you. How can I help you? How can I bless you? Enemies? I don't have any; how could I? Just for a moment, can you feel that? That's how God turns the world from evil to love. This is the real God. This is the God you can trust. This is the real story of love because God is love!

Tell me about the god you don't believe in because I probably don't believe in him either! That's what this old preacher said on Moody Radio. The real living God is all about love, and out of love, He saves us, sings over us, delights in us, and calls us His children. He says, "Call me Daddy. Don't call me 'mean father,' but rather call me Daddy, Pappa, a loving term."

I had a stoic father, but he had a love that was obvious in his actions. He always showed up, always took us to our baseball games. Dad learned the game since he didn't know it as an immigrant. This man could not be stopped. Orphaned by World War II, he put himself into boarding school. He tried to practice baseball with us, although his massive Popeye-like forearms could not hit the ball softly. Whack! He used this massive baseball bat with one hand, his arms strong from twisting wrenches as an auto mechanic. "Catch the darn thing," he would say. He and my mom would take us to church every Sunday and go to our school presentations. He was our scoutmaster in boy scouts. He taught us to work on our own cars. And he wouldn't take a dime that wasn't his! He always went to work ten minutes early and always left ten minutes after quitting time. He was never late, never took advantage, no matter who was looking or not looking. He and my mother flew to Florida to see me in college. We flew to Parris Island, South Carolina, to see my two brothers complete their boot-camp training as United States Marines. He helped us with our houses, helped us with our cars, boats, children, everything. He didn't say it much, but his actions all pointed to love.

That's what the cross shows. Try to comprehend what level of love for you God has that He would pour out His wrath on His Son for you! His actions say it all.

My wife is reading *The Reason for God* by Timothy Keller, and she read me a few pieces, so I know I want to read his book. He sounds like Max Lucado, just gifted to state things so plainly that we can understand. Timothy Keller writes:

> *If God had not allowed Joseph's years of suffering, he never would have been such a powerful agent for social justice and spiritual healing. Whenever I preach on this text, I hear from many people who identify with that narrative. Many people have to admit that most of what they really needed for success in life came to them through their most difficult and painful experiences [...]*

> *If you have a God great and transcendent enough to be mad at because He hasn't stopped evil and suffering in the world, then you have (at the same moment) a God great and transcendent enough to have good reasons for allowing it to continue that you can't know. Indeed, you can't have it both ways.*[3]

Keller quotes Philosopher J. L. Mackie in his book *The Miracle of Theism*. Mackie says: "Just because you can't see or imagine a good reason why God might allow something to happen doesn't mean there can't be one."[4]

---

[3] Timothy Keller, *The Reason for God* (Penguin Publishing Group, 2018), 24.
[4] Timothy Keller, *The Miracle of Theism* (Oxford, 1982), 23.

And what God says we can bank on is this: "And we know that in all things God works for the good of those who love him, who have been called according to his purpose" (Romans 8:28). Bank on that! In *all* things, God works for the good of those who love Him.

The other thing that was mentioned by our small group Friday night was this: remember how many times God has come through for you. That's really what this book is, a small portion of what God has done for me and some others.

I know our oldest son questioned what in the world we did back when he was younger. Hopefully, this book will help him and all of you who read it see that we did everything to try and follow what the God of the universe was guiding us, by His Holy Spirit, to do. Here are a few zillion other amazing things God did over those past ten years when I did not make the money needed for our house, but instead, we attempted to follow what God said. Let me repeat that: over those ten years, I did not make the money needed for the house. In fact, for the first three and a half years, I made *zero*. And spoiler alert: God always provided!

I wish I could say I didn't waver, but you already heard that I wavered last week, so no sense faking it now! But I'm getting better. We're in a tough but blessed season, and we praise God no matter what now. I'm not pretending, but sometimes you also have to speak the positive forward, and then the positive moves forward. Believe it in your heart and say it out loud with your mouth.

Just like when my wife said, "We already prayed for God to open the door. Since He wants to do this, let's pray for the next step! He already confirmed He wants to do this."

So, that's what we did back in 2002, and you also heard the circumstances and miracles leading up to 2002.

PEACE THAT GOES BEYOND THE CIRCUMSTANCES

When my wife said to pray that next prayer of faith in 2002, something happened spiritually. I was ready to move forward, but a married couple is no longer two people. It is now one beautiful new creation of God, and when we both hear from heaven, we can't be stopped.

So, we prayed that God would give us the next step and thanked Him for His goodness, and even though I could see the mountain of things in front of us, we had such peace that God would give us the next step that we left the prayer in God's hands and went out for a peaceful bike ride. Great is the mountain if you focus on it, but greater is the peace if you ask the Lord to move your mountain and trust Him by faith that He will. Jesus said it this way in Philippians 4:6–7:

Do not be anxious about anything, but in every situation, by prayer and petition, with thanksgiving, present your requests to God. And the peace of God, which transcends all understanding, will guard your hearts and your minds in Christ Jesus.

We sort of did that: we prayed and asked, thanking Him for His goodness. And this peace, which didn't make sense, came over us. Really! If you knew how much of a work-at-it type of personality I am, you would realize what a big deal that was. I would normally get right to "task mode." If there is a task to be done, there is no question about what to do—the task! But somehow, I just knew God had this covered. So, I didn't really have a task to do; He did. So, this peace, which didn't match the circumstances, came over us, and we went out for an awesome peaceful bike ride.

When we returned from the bike ride, I felt this faith rising up inside of me. So confident was I that God would now reveal His next steps, I took out a notebook and a pen and said," Okay, God, let me have it." What He poured out was amazing: a high-level vision and strategy for a fiber-to-the-home company, with a diagram and a list of names of ten people.

Miracle 31. God pours out a high-level plan for a company He wants us to create and aim for after we pray for His next step.

I remember asking for prayer in our weekly Bible study after worship that next Sunday. The first thing someone said when I told them God was calling us to start a company was, "How will you make money? What is your business plan?" I said, "I have no idea; all I know is God said to do it." (That's one reason why I was asking for prayer!)

With other faithful people praying, the right foundation was in place (at least for that day!), and we could expect God to move now. One of the names on the list was Scott Allen Wenzel. Scott Allen, his wife, Regina, and their wonderful little boy, Stephan, previously lived in Florida and traveled west for a job in California. But while they were still on the way, the job became no longer available, so he had to suddenly take a job in Phoenix, working for a construction company. I remember that prayer request and hardship as they were traveling. Since now God said to call people on the list He gave me for the fiber company, I called Scott Allen.

I told Scott Allen about the fiber-to-the-home company God called me to start and the vision for it. What he told me in return was incredible!

"Wow, you might want to sit down, Rich! The construction company I work for is called Fishel, and we install fiber in the ground."

I said, "Wow, that's awesome!"

He said, "Wait, there's more; we want startups and other fiber-to-the-home companies to thrive, so we have business plans and other docs to help."

"Hallelujah, praise God!"

"Wait: even more. I'm moving back to Florida, and you're going to be in my territory!"

"You mean you have business plans and help for fiber-to-the-home companies, and you will be back here in Florida, and it's your job to put me in business?"

"Yes, that's right!"

Wow, that's God—more than we can even ask or imagine! Ephesians 3:20–21 says:

> *Now to him who is able to do immeasurably more than all we ask or imagine, according to his power that is at work within us, to him be glory in the church and in Christ Jesus throughout all generations, for ever and ever! Amen.*

Miracle 32. God orchestrates Scott Allen's life to be a help to this fiber-to-the-home company in many of the pieces of the puzzle.

That Sunday, after church, we went to Chili's to meet some friends for lunch. This guy named Keith Elliott comes over and reintroduces himself. He says, "Hi, I'm Keith Elliott, and I'm sorry I don't remember your name." We both worked at Paradyne. I remember him from Paradyne and say hi to him, reminding him of my name. We chat, and I mention I have just lost my job. "Best thing that ever happened to you!" he says with confidence. "Why?" I say. He says, "I lost my job, and I've been working for the Lord ever since." Wow, I'm getting ready to start a company that God said to start, and God puts this guy right in front of me!

So, Keith and I talked and had lunch the following Thursday, where the Lord made clear this calling is for a telecom company with more than just networking. We must control the content in the pipe by owning the pipe. That's why the Lord revealed the fiber-to-the-home vision!

At lunch on Thursday, Keith also told me he and Heidi had trouble the previous Sunday with the kids and wanted to go home, but God told him to go to Chili's to meet someone. So, they went to Chili's in obedience. When Heidi saw me, she asked, "You know him, do you remember his name?" and he said, "No, but I'm not going to let that stop me. God said I'm here to meet someone, so maybe it's him." That's when he got up and reintroduced himself to me, even though he didn't remember my name!

Miracle 33. God sends Keith and Heidi to Chili's to meet me to deliver the message that working for the Lord is good and help solidify the telecom company is what God is pointing to.

On September 3, 2002, I met with Ken, director of affiliate relations for the Christian Television Network Inc. (CTN), and he indicated that if we put the fiber-to-the-home network in, he expected they would provide content! He said he would give this vision to the prayer coordinator. No contract was signed, of course, but it was very encouraging that he was already thinking yes after he heard the details of the vision. This was even before the company was formed. On September 4, 2002, the next day, the Lord revealed Alpha Fiber was the name of the Lord's company. Later, we negotiated and put in place an agreement to carry two of their channels. A great start for Christian content along our fiber!

Most people, including me, did not understand why God would call a person to start a for-profit company. Looking back on it now, I can say that one main reason is *people*. God is always interested in reaching people (see 1 Timothy 2:3), and just about every time someone asked me about Alpha Fiber, I told them it was a company that God started. That almost always led to a discussion about God and how He talks to us, who He is, etc. Hundreds or maybe over a thousand people heard the good news of Jesus Christ because of this.

In September of 2002, young people of Jehovah's Witnesses came to our door, and I asked them what they believed. They handed me a pamphlet but couldn't tell me what it said. I guess that kicked off a report back to someone because next, a woman named Gayle came, and we had an interesting discussion at the door, but she couldn't answer all my questions about what scriptures she was referring to. A week or so later, she came back with someone named Nick, and we talked about their beliefs.

Nick made appointments to come back many times over the next several months as we sat down and went through some of the details. He said they don't believe that Jesus is God. I prayed a lot about what Nick said because it didn't match with what is in the Bible. Nick was saying not to worship Jesus but only Jehovah, God the Father. But Revelation 1:5–6 says:

> *And from Jesus Christ, who is the faithful witness, the firstborn from the dead, and the ruler of the kings of the earth. To him who loves us and has freed us from our sins by his blood, and has made us to be a kingdom and priests to serve his God and Father—to him be glory and power for ever and ever! Amen.*

So, giving glory to Jesus is called for. Also, Jesus is the Word, according to John 1:1, so using the Word to keep Jesus from getting the glory due Him didn't sound right. After a few more visits, in August of 2003, the Lord showed me quite a few verses confirming Jesus is God. In Colossians 2:9–10, it says: "For in Christ all the fullness of the Deity lives in bodily form, and in Christ you have been brought to fullness. He is the head over every power and authority."

Also, Jesus, the Lamb of God, is worthy to receive honor and glory, as Revelation 5:12–13 states very clearly:

> *In a loud voice they were saying: "Worthy is the Lamb, who was slain, to receive power and wealth and wisdom and strength and honor and glory and praise!"*

> *Then I heard every creature in heaven and on earth and under the earth and on the sea, and all that is in them, saying: "To him who sits on the throne and to the Lamb be praise and honor and glory and power, for ever and ever!"*

On August 20, 2003 (this is almost a full year later), I prayed that the Lord make a way if He wanted me to give Nick this message. And He did! Nick called that same day and asked to come over with Fred, their bishop for the area.

Miracle 34. God arranges for Nick and Fred to come to receive the message He has given me.

When they arrived, Nick said, "Rich, I've done a lot of talking. Is there anything you'd like to say to us?" Talk about a setup! Wow, God is good. All the time! (Promise Keepers again.)

Miracle 35. God arranges for Nick and Fred to ask if I have anything to say to them, just when I have something from the Lord to say to them.

So, I told them. I had to! The Word makes it clear: if you don't think Jesus is worthy of worship, you don't know Him and are not reading the Word (He is the Word; see John 1:1). We talked about the scriptures I was pointed to and their importance, but Nick did not seem happy that this came up in front of Fred. After that, I never saw Nick again. I later heard he had some medical problems and died. God, in His mercy, gave Nick the clear message that Jesus *is* the right and only way to get to Jehovah God and that He is worthy of our worship.

That was a year after starting the company, but that first year did not go by so fast. I tried to start every day with prayer and reading of the Word. I needed to hear from heaven to try and implement whatever God had in mind. This was no easy task for me. We don't hear with our ears, nor do we see a blueprint or a spreadsheet with our eyes. Instead, we see through a glass dimly lit (1 Corinthians 13:12), meaning everything is not entirely clear with a full business plan and a three-to-five-year projection. Instead, the Word is a lamp to my feet and a light to my path (Psalm 119:105), meaning the Word will show the next step or two forward. So, I definitely needed to check the Word every single day for the next step or two while trying to edit, update, and execute a solid business plan.

At this point, the company didn't have funding to do anything. I spent that year writing and editing a business plan and showing it to potential investors. But I also wasn't making any money! I didn't even collect unemployment because they said if you are working anywhere, even at your own business, full time, you can't collect unemployment, even if there is no sign of money for many months to come.

While trying to provide for a wife and three kids, trying to be faithful, and trying to get a business off the ground the way God wanted it and for whatever reasons He had in mind, I was trying to keep sane. I can't tell you how nerve-racking that was: to feel the pressure to provide and not have something coming in! I know some of you understand that.

As a result, I was also out doing a little computer-networking service, trying to make a dollar. But the company was a C corporation, and the expenses far exceeded the $200 or so that came into the company occasionally. I hadn't earned any money (at all) this whole time. I wasn't able to take a penny in salary. But somehow, God kept paying our bills. I can't tell you all the ways God intervened, but sometimes I wrote down specifics.

On August 16, 2003, I wrote, "When I felt the oil was getting low (I'll explain that in a minute), Beckie and I prayed for God to provide and for God to guide us: Should we sell the house now that values are up? Should we sell the boat? Refinance? What?"

What I meant by "the oil was getting low" was a reference to 1 Kings 17:14, which says: "For this is what the Lord, the God of Israel, says: 'The jar of flour will not be used up and the jug of oil will not run dry until the day the Lord sends rain on the land.'"

It's an amazing story of God's miraculous provisions for a single mom in need. And this became the foundational verse for this financial faith-walk season of our lives. God said, "The oil will not run out!" This reaching out to God for provisions caused me to check and see if there was any "oil" in any small jars lying around. I had some stock in a previous company that I worked for that had become virtually worthless. It was less than 1 percent of what it used to be. But the day that I needed it, it was up high enough to pay the mortgage. It had returned to a small part of its value!

Miracle 36. God miraculously raises a worthless stock to a high enough value to pay the mortgage.

Now, I didn't write all the details of every miracle provision every day. I was too busy working, praying, listening, fathering, husbanding (is that a word?), but I did not get paid one penny for three and a half years during that time. Every monthly mortgage and utility and food bill payment was miraculous. That's forty-two months! So those are really *miracle* numbers thirty-six through seventy-seven!

Let me note, from memory, some of them here:

More than a few times, we went to a local food bank and picked up a box of food. While we were there, we encouraged and prayed for and with some of the workers who sometimes see only struggling, desperate people. We also encouraged and prayed with some of the struggling people who came there.

At least four times, a zero-interest credit card came in the mail, just in time to pay off the previous one. I had a small amount of gold, and it shot up in price, just in time to pay some bills.

We reduced expenses by refinancing the house to a lower interest rate by getting an adjustable mortgage. That was a risk because rates could have gone up a short time later. Instead, rates continued holding steady or going down, and not up, almost the entire time, across the next twenty years!

At least three times, people gave us money (for us, not for the ministry as was later) because God put it on their hearts. I know that doesn't seem to account for all forty-two months, but somehow it did. God just did it!

Read 1 Kings 17 for yourself. God really means that He is able to take care of us. The bank account got low, but the funds (the oil) never ran out. They just didn't; I can't explain how: God just did it. A life verse for us is: "And my God will meet all your needs according to the riches of his glory in Christ Jesus" (Philippians 4:19).

You see, God doesn't meet our needs according to crumbs that fall from His table. No, instead, He meets our needs according to the riches of His glory in Christ Jesus. My God owns everything in the world, and He loves me! And He leads me down a path, but I don't have to worry (though I did many, many, many times, honestly).

The prince (or for a woman—princess) does not have to walk around with cash in his pocket or even a credit card. He is well cared for and has everything he needs. For anything that he wants, he merely asks. That's us as children of God! But we have to believe it, pray as we believe it, speak as we believe it, by faith! Do you believe it?

Another life verse is Proverbs 3:5–6 (the comment in brackets is mine):

> *Trust in the Lord with all your heart and lean not on your own understanding; in all your ways submit to him [or "acknowledge Him," the King James Version says], and he will make your paths straight.*

I don't always understand the path; you can't use human logic alone to make decisions. But my path is straight if I'm trusting Him with all my heart, submitting to Him, and acknowledging Him in all my ways.

On August 26, 2003, I went to a woman named Diane to help with her home computer. She asked me about Alpha Fiber, and I told her God started the company. (I told you: God used that to reach many, many people.) She asked me all sorts of questions, like, "How did God tell you to start a company?" and "How do you know what He wants?" I felt led to show her the scriptures that helped me. I asked her if she had a Bible and asked her to bring it to me.

I showed her one or two scriptures in her Bible. And then I felt something bubbling up inside me all at once: I had to show her, point her, to Him. I turned to Ephesians 2:10 and explained to her that I do certain things that God prepared for me to do in advance. That means God had a plan for certain things, and He created me to do them! Then I showed her that those good works don't save me; only faith in what Jesus did on the cross can save me or anyone.

Then I asked her, "Have you ever done that?"

"Done what?" she asked.

"Put your faith in what Jesus did on the cross to forgive your sins and made Him leader of your life?"

And she said, "No, I haven't."

So, I said, "Would you like to?"

"Now?"

"Yes, that's why I'm here! That's one of the good works that God prepared for me to do in advance: be here to tell you about Jesus and how He died for you to save you!"

And she said, "Yes, I would like that!"

So, Diane received Jesus as her Lord and Savior because of what God did to start Alpha Fiber. I didn't do a thing but show up and listen to His voice and move my lips every now and then. It was awesome; what a rush! God arranged all of these circumstances, and He did that many times!

Miracle 78. God orchestrates and draws Diane near and grants her salvation.

Have you read Ephesians 2:8–10?

> *For it is by grace you have been saved, through faith—and this is not from yourselves, it is the gift of God—not by works, so that no one can boast. For we are God's handiwork, created in Christ Jesus to do good works, which God prepared in advance for us to do.*

More importantly, have you put your faith in this grace? This gift of God that, by faith in what Jesus did on the cross, you can have all of your sins forgiven and removed; you can be saved forever and brought back to a right relationship with God the Father?

God says it this way with three scriptures in Romans (often called the Roman Road to salvation):

My paraphrase with the scriptures next to them:

1. All are sinners and can't be with God. "All have sinned and fall short of the glory of God" (Romans 3:23).

2. The punishment for sin is death, so that's what all people who ever lived deserve. "The wages of sin is death" (Romans 6:23a).

3. But Jesus lived a sinless life so He could be the death that God requires for sin in our place. Then He got up after being dead,

proving everything He said is true and proving He has control even over death. So, He offers us eternal life. "But the gift of God is eternal life in Christ Jesus our Lord" (Romans 6:23b).

4. If you believe that all the way, so you're not afraid to say it but rather can't contain it, you're saved forever! "If you declare with your mouth, 'Jesus is Lord,' and believe in your heart that God raised him from the dead, you will be saved" (Romans 10:9).

Please don't forget all the evidence that proves way beyond reasonable doubt that Jesus died, was buried, and was raised from the dead. Also, just look up in the sky: Who lights all those candles every night and makes sure they are in the exact same place? How is that even possible?

Psalm 19:1–4 says:

The heavens declare the glory of God; the skies proclaim the work of his hands. Day after day they pour forth speech; night after night they reveal knowledge. They have no speech, they use no words; no sound is heard from them. Yet their voice goes out into all the earth, their words to the ends of the world.

How about you? All you have to do is, by faith, turn to Jesus, believe, and receive. Believe that Jesus died in your place and was raised from the dead and surrender the leadership role of your life over to the Creator of life; that is, make Jesus your leader and Lord of everything. With that one belief, decision, and commitment, you are instantly and forever saved and are now a child of God. Born new, or born again, as Jesus said to Nicodemus. Read John 3, verses 1 through 21 here and see what you think:

Now there was a Pharisee, a man named Nicodemus who was a member of the Jewish ruling council. He came to Jesus at night and said, "Rabbi, we know that you are a teacher who has come from God. For no one could perform the signs you are doing if God were not with him." Jesus replied, "Very truly I tell you, no one can see the kingdom of God unless they are born again." "How can someone be born when they are old?" Nicodemus asked. "Surely they cannot enter a second time into their mother's womb to be born!"

Jesus answered, "Very truly I tell you, no one can enter the kingdom of God unless they are born of water and the Spirit. Flesh gives birth to flesh, but the Spirit gives birth to spirit. You should not be surprised at my saying, 'You must be born again.' The wind blows wherever it pleases. You hear its sound, but you cannot tell where it comes from or where it is going. So it is with everyone born of the Spirit."

"How can this be?" Nicodemus asked. "You are Israel's teacher," said Jesus, "and do you not understand these things? Very truly I tell you, we speak of what we know, and we testify to what we have seen, but still you people do not accept our testimony. I have spoken to you of earthly things and you do not believe; how then will you believe if I speak of heavenly things? No one has ever gone into heaven except the one who came from heaven—the Son of Man. Just as Moses lifted up the snake in the wilderness, so the Son of Man must be lifted up, that everyone who believes may have eternal life in him."

For God so loved the world that he gave his one and only Son, that whoever believes in him shall not perish but have eternal life. For God did not send his Son into the world to condemn the world, but to save the world through him. Whoever believes in him is not condemned, but whoever does not believe stands condemned already because they have not believed in the name of God's one and only Son. This is the verdict: Light has come into the world, but people loved darkness instead of light because their deeds were evil. Everyone who does evil hates the light, and will not come into the light for fear that their deeds will be exposed. But whoever lives by the truth comes into the light, so that it may be seen plainly that what they have done has been done in the sight of God.

I thank God that everyone who reads this book responds to the calling and invitation of Jesus and God the Father and the Holy Spirit, which you just read. Some for a reminder and encouragement, and some for the first time. Today, since you just heard His voice, do not take a hard stand against it, but instead, be wide open to Him and this amazing gift.

TEACH

In September of 2003, I felt like God wanted me to teach one day, maybe in the Sunday school class that we were attending. Marti Giancola was leading the class at that time, and she mentioned she needed help so she could focus on other things. I thought that if I studied hard for another year or two, maybe I could start to apprentice or something if that was God's will. (I know some of you are laughing right now; you should be!)

As it turned out, Marti told Beckie she wanted to talk to me about helping out in the class, and I told Beckie I had felt God call me to that. When I told Marti the next Sunday at class, she announced to the class that I was taking over next week!

"Next week? No, no, no," I said, "I'm just a Dumbo Columbo right now; I need a few years to study so I can do this."

And Marti put her hand on my shoulder, smiled, and said, "Rich, you don't do it: God does it. You just have to be available to Him and trust Him."

"What? How will I know what to say and study and look at each week? God will do that?"

She answered that He would.

"Well, if God will do that, then I'll do it. But I will not fake it! He will have to give it to me, every time!"

And He did! I don't know how else to say that to you. God did! He provided the topic and pointed me to the scriptures, gave me the words, and then we would discuss it as a group. And He would speak up through other people in the class, and we would all learn of Him. It was amazing! I would seek Him every morning in my normal daily time with Him, and He would give me stuff.

One week, God didn't give me anything during the week. I would normally have something that He pointed to by Wednesday or Thursday morning, and He would refine it by Friday. But this week, I had nothing, and it was Thursday afternoon. I got nothing, and we were heading somewhere Saturday early, so I knew the time would be rushed. I started to panic but prayed, "Please give me something, Lord, but even if You don't, I know You can do it at any time." Well, I had nothing, and Saturday night came. Should I stay up all night or trust Him for it on the way to church? I decided if He could hold the universe together, He could make the desks cry out on the spot if He wanted to.

So, I told the class, "Sorry, God did not give me anything to study today, but He can give it to us now on the spot, so let's pray that He does." When we were done praying, I said something like, "Last week we were in the book of Isaiah, chapter…; turn now to the book…, chapter…" Words and scriptures just flowed into the back of my head and came out of my mouth.

When the class was over, some new people said they thought it was a very good Bible study, and they thanked me. I said, "Don't thank me; I just moved my lips. Thank the Lord: He's the one who did it all! You heard me say I had nothing." Then I asked someone for a copy of the notes they took because, for the first time, I did not have one note on what we talked about.

Miracle 79. God miraculously feeds me an entire Bible study lesson in real time while I am standing in front of the class.

Another time in the Sunday Bible study class, Nancy Wilder (now Ostneberg) brought her son Justin because he had a fever. But not just any fever. Nancy, Justin, and his brother, Chris, had been in Massachusetts on vacation when Justin developed a fever of 106 degrees after having an upset stomach. The fever subsided that night but shot up again the next day and every day after that for the next month. After a few days of these life-threatening high fevers (106 is dangerous for anyone), Nancy took him to the hospital, but they could find no explanation for the fevers. The doctors instructed her to treat him with dual medications of ibuprofen (Advil) and acetaminophen

(Tylenol), as well as tepid baths and ice packs on his head. But the fevers persisted, so Nancy took Justin to Children's Hospital in Boston, one of the premier children's hospitals in the world, where he was tested for every possible cause of the illness and seen by teams of world-class doctors. The doctors were confounded because nothing was out of range on any of the tests. Yet the fevers persisted.

Justin developed a rash all over, from head to toe and even on the palms of his hands, but nothing the doctors prescribed provided relief. He had also taken on a peculiar grayish cast to his skin all over. And the fevers continued every day and night. But Justin never lost faith that God would heal him, and he said so to his mother. Over the new few weeks, Nancy decided they would fly home to Florida. Upon arriving back in Florida, they went to All Children's Hospital in St. Petersburg for more tests and visits to specialist after specialist, but still, the doctors could not identify what was wrong with Justin. He saw twenty-three doctors and teams of specialists in all.

After forty-five days of this illness, Nancy brought Justin to the Sunday school class, so we could lay hands on him and pray for his healing, as the Bible outlines. Dr. Norma Neal Gause, then in her eighties, was in class that day. She was an awesome woman of God and a learned woman with a PhD in theology. She was also an associate professor of literature at the university level, a professor of religion, and the dean of students at a local college, and she founded the Suncoast Bible Study in the 1970s, where she taught and mentored for over thirty years.

We sat Justin in a chair, gathered around him, gently put hands on his shoulders, and started to pray for his healing. Norma Neal walked through the group up to Justin. She anointed him with oil with the sign of the cross on his forehead and then said, "There's a spirit of infirmity," and she asked Justin to look at her. Then she looked him in the eyes and commanded the spirit of infirmity to leave Justin in the name of Jesus. She told him if he felt like throwing up, that would be okay and might or might not happen.

One week later to the day, the color came back to Justin's skin, the rash faded away, and the fever left him, never to return. The illness had lasted a total of fifty-two days. What an amazing healing God delivered to Justin!

We looked up in the Bible for a reference to a spirit of infirmity. In Luke 13:10, we are told there is a woman who has a spirit of infirmity that has her crippled in a bent-over position. Jesus lays hands on her and speaks to her and says, "Woman, thou art loosed from thine infirmity" (Luke 13:12, KJV). And she suddenly straightens up and is healed.

During another Sunday Bible study class, I felt like the Lord said, "Take this outside." I prayed about it and then asked the class to pray about it. In the service that day, the Lord made clear, through the sermon, His desire for us to go out into the community and pour love on people and pray for people in His name. We were to be prepared for whatever He might do.

We planned to go the following week out to the Sponge Docks, the local tourist attraction area for Tarpon Springs along the Anclote River, where we have a number of sponge-diving boats that go out and return with these aquatic animals (yes, sponges from the ocean are actually animals). We also have a number of restaurants and souvenir shops there, making it a perfect place to hear what the Spirit of God is whispering and then do what He says.

We were studying the book of Acts, and in chapter 8 verse 26, Philip is directed to go south to a road, and we felt directed to go to the Sponge Docks area (road). While Philip was there, the Spirit told Philip to go over to a chariot and stay near it. When Philip did that, he heard the person inside reading the book of Isaiah, and Philip knew what God wanted him to do. He asked the person if he understood what he was reading, and being invited in, Philip explained to him the gospel of Jesus outlined in that section of Isaiah. Then Philip baptized him when they came to some water!

It was that simple. Our plan was to pray, and then we were to do whatever the Spirit of God told each one of us to do while we were there and available to God. It was awesome!

A few of us felt led to go into a store that was doing some sort of palm-reading nonsense. Those of us who felt we were sent in there lovingly talked to the woman behind the counter. She asked where we came from, and we told her, "The local church," and that God sent us into her store. We asked her if she had any prayer requests, and she started to tear up and explain her mother's medical urgency. She seemed touched by the thought that God sent us, but she didn't say it out loud. We prayed for her and her mother right there, and then we walked around the building, praying for God to come in like a flood and have His way, pour out His love, draw her near, and grant her salvation, in Jesus's name. We asked Him to close the doors of that place, since divination does not please God, and instead give her a vision for a different type of business, and then we tried our best to pour love on her some more before we left.

Our job is simple: we do the going, praying, and loving part. God's job is the heavy lifting: He orchestrates events, delivers healings, softens hearts, sends His servants, draws people near, and grants them salvation!

Two weeks later, I went back into the store to check on her and her mother, and she was so thankful we prayed and came in to see her. We once again gave credit to Jesus, attempting to point her to the source of everything: our reason for coming in and her mother's reason for getting any better. She said her mother was unexpectedly doing much better. Two months later, the store was closed. I'm not sure where she went, but I'm certain God can reach her in His love and point her to the path of life.

Roy Wenzel also felt the Lord lead him to talk to someone, but he was led to a big bad-looking biker dude walking down the Sponge Docks with his girl on his arm. Roy took a deep breath and walked slowly, respectfully, but directly up to the biker guy. "Excuse me," Roy said with his great Chicago accent, "but can I ask you a question?" The biker just lowered his sunglasses a bit down his nose and looked down at Roy (key word "down": he was a big guy) over his shades with a bit of a stern look. "Do you know Jesus to be your Lord and Savior?" Roy said. Wow, I might have started with something a little more subtle, but Roy was led to go right for the heart! The biker's facial expression lightened, and he said in a deep voice, "Why, yes, I do. Thank you for asking!" And with that, he raised his shades back up and walked on. Roy walked on, too, thankful that he made it through the event with all his limbs still intact.

Most of the rest of the class reported that they were led to pray for people as they walked by them, and the Lord prompted them. It felt so good to have the courage to actually go when the Lord said, "Go," and to be available to Him for anything He wanted to do.

Are you available to the Lord? Would you actually go somewhere if He sent you?

Bruce Wilkinson wrote a few great books that illustrate this point. Maybe you remember the craze that hit regarding one of his books called *The Prayer of Jabez*. Jabez is a little story tucked away inside the book of 1 Chronicles in the Bible. Many people breeze right through it (or skip it altogether) because it is mostly a book listing the genealogy of people and the kings who ruled over Israel. Who wants to read the list of names when we just finished reading the actual history, with names of the kings of Israel in the previous two books: 1 Kings and 2 Kings? But if you skip or breeze through any part of the living Word of God, you might miss what I call a "golden nugget."

Well, tucked in 1 Chronicles 4 is a nugget in verse 9 that Bruce Wilkinson wrote about in his book. It names Jabez but then describes how he defied his name. In those days, your name was basically your destiny, and his name meant "pain"! But he instead prays for God to bless him and not just bless him a little. He prays for God to bless him a lot. He also prays for God to expand his territory for God. Bruce Wilkinson wrote that we should all be asking God to expand our territory or do more through us for Him.

People everywhere were praying for God to use them to expand their territory of influencing people so they could influence more people for God. And they reported many God-orchestrated moments, but they weren't sure what to do about them.

Given so many reports like that, Bruce Wilkinson wrote *You Were Born for This*. A book that basically describes what to do next. It describes that we were created by God to deliver miracle messages, and if we listened to the "nudge" (I love that he didn't use theological jargon) from God, as Philip did in Acts 8, we too would be used by God.

We studied the book *You Were Born for This* in our class too, and I highly recommend it. It's the reason why I felt led, or nudged, to go to the mall one afternoon. I felt like I was sent to the food area, and once there, I was supposed to say something to a waitress that the Lord pointed to while I was praying. I wasn't quite sure what God wanted to say, and I noticed she kept her head down while she cleaned off the tables in this food-court area.

I prayed some more and finished my sandwich, and then I felt a nudge to give her the cash I had in my pocket. I asked the Lord to confirm that I was hearing Him right, and He did, so I walked over to where she was cleaning and tried to talk to her. But she couldn't speak English. A manager-type young man in the same uniform walked over and asked what I needed. I asked him if it was okay if I gave her a tip. I felt really weird because there was nothing powerful yet that was going on; it seemed like some weirdo hitting on one of the girls or something.

He translated what I said into Spanish, and she shrugged her shoulders and nodded. Just then, God started whispering into the back of my head, as I like to refer to it. He said to tell her, "Maybe you want to get some lunch for yourself. You see people eat here all the time." And as the young man translated, she started to look puzzled. "And you don't think anyone even sees you," God continued. "But God sees you, and He sent me here to tell you that. He sees you, and He loves you." At this point, as the young man translated, her puzzled look dissolved, and she started to tear up and cry. Now she was looking at me and looking at the translator and looking back at me with teary eyes wide with amazement as if she was thinking, *How do you know?*

I didn't hear anything else from the Lord, so I didn't say anything else. I've (sometimes) learned not to add anything if God doesn't add to it. Then I just smiled and said goodbye and walked out of the food-court area. As I did, I prayed for the Lord to draw her closer and comfort her because, obviously, there was something going on in her life. How cool that He reached down from heaven to give her a message of encouragement!

What about you? Are you available to God at all? In order to be available to the Lord, we can't have our schedules packed to overflowing. It can't be a twenty-minute drive if you need to be there in fifteen minutes! You know what I mean? We are not available for even an obvious need at that point, like a person hit by a car right in front of us, let alone the Spirit of God saying, "Go over near that place," as He did to Philip. Would you commit to a schedule with fewer things so that there is room for God to move in your life and through your life? How else will you stop and serve God by helping someone?

Do you think maybe God doesn't intervene in the affairs of people on the earth? In 2 Chronicles 18:18, God decides it's time for the wicked king Ahab to go, and He has a sort of meeting in heaven. He's actually open to suggestions from the angelic attendees! The decision comes down that they will send some lying prophets to lie to Ahab. Now, in this case, that's a negative outcome, but nonetheless, that is God intervening in the affairs of people on the earth in order for His will, the end of Ahab, to be accomplished. He can do it any way He wants, but for some reason, God chooses to use us, His servants, to implement some of His blessings in this world. And we are blessed by it too! That's the double blessing that only God can accomplish.

Blessings also came from teaching younger people. When Beckie and I felt certain the Lord wanted us to homeschool our kids, it was because the public-school system was failing all three of our children and focusing more on education for sex rather than reading, writing, and math. Homeschooling opened up a new door of blessing others and being blessed. We not only taught our little loves at home, but the Lord put on Beckie's heart and the heart of a few other people to start a Christian homeschool co-op. There wasn't one in our immediate area, and the Lord arranged the pieces after the team of founders began to pray. These people did such a fantastic job of pulling this together, by God's grace and orchestration, and with their years of continuous prayer and hard work.

People like Nicole Kerr, my wife, Beckie, and many others founded the co-op and created a beautiful place for Christian homeschooling families to grow, learn, and thrive. Mazzie was instrumental in helping because she had already started a homeschool co-op elsewhere. God used this group of people to birth Lighthouse Christian Homeschool Academy! And what a blessing it has been to so many families, with rigorous academics from loving, talented parents as teachers and other teachers. God blessed it so much that we had attorneys, music teachers, biologists teaching biology, engineers, former public-school math teachers, art teachers, sports, skits, you name it. Oh, to pour into a young heart and mind and let them know they are awesome because they are made by an awesome God, who doesn't make any mistakes, is soul-enriching to both the encourager and the encouraged.

Do you pour into anyone as the Lord leads you? If you have the gift of teaching (Romans 12:6 and 1 Corinthians 12:28), do you teach anyone? It is not just a form of giving, but there is a great reward in your soul.

I was blessed to be able to teach some science classes, like high-school chemistry, as our oldest hit the high school years, and computer classes from basics through advanced. My wife and I also taught a movie-creation-basics class—that was a lot of fun, and she taught English, writing, literature, and journalism.

Later, I was called to teach technology, using my design-engineering background in communications and networking. I taught adults the basics of networking for AT&T and other telecom companies. A new company benefit allowed the laborers, like pole climbers and cable installers, to take networking classes paid for by the company.

Since I had designed networking boxes, both hardware and software, I was also asked to create a Cisco certification class from scratch so that this training company could have its own. I read a few Cisco books on their level one and level two Cisco certifications (called CCENT and CCNA) and created the curriculum—presentations, workbooks, chapter tests—everything. Then I taught it to the students who had successfully taken and passed the introductory networking classes that I taught.

The Lord used even that season to message people because He always had me on the lookout for someone who was seeking Him. One time after the class, as I packed a bunch of routers and other equipment back into my truck, a young man asked me if we could talk. He could tell from the examples I used and the occasional mention that I knew something about God. He asked me what he should do about a family problem, something about his mother-in-law now needing a place to stay, but he was already having marital problems. I prayed with him right there, and as best I could, I pointed him to the scriptures that I could think of, after explaining to him that God is the one with the answers and that He is able to make a way when there even seems to be no way; He specializes in that.

I remember driving back, being encouraged that God used me again, and I felt a leading to stop the car and go to a restaurant. I was really tired after the full day: these were night classes that went from 6 p.m. till 10 p.m., and I worked during the day from eight to five. That's why I shook it off and didn't stop. I rationalized that there was no one obvious in need of help that I could see and that maybe I was just imagining things. I didn't pray and ask; I just drove on. As I did, I felt strongly that I missed it; I missed the opportunity to do something that the Lord wanted.

I now try not to make quick decisions like that without praying, even if I am tired: who knows what life needs to hear from heaven.

HUNDREDFOLD

In September of 2003, we committed to tithing on a high salary to come for the next year. Now, I was making a salary of zero dollars in 2003 (and I made zero dollars in salary in 2004 too), but we were hearing and trusting God for a high salary that would come. What I later found out is that Jesus says (I didn't know it at the time) in Mark 10:29–30 (KJV):

And Jesus answered and said, Verily I say unto you, There is no man that hath left house, or brethren, or sisters, or father, or mother, or wife, or children, or lands, for my sake, and the gospel's, But he shall receive an hundredfold now in this time, houses, and brethren, and sisters, and mothers, and children, and lands, with persecutions; and in the world to come eternal life.

And in Matthew 19:29, Jesus says:

And everyone who has left houses or brothers or sisters or father or mother or wife or children or fields for my sake will receive a hundred times as much and will inherit eternal life.

And in Luke 18:29–30:

"Truly I tell you," Jesus said to them, "no one who has left home or wife or brothers or sisters or parents or children for the sake of the kingdom of God will fail to receive many times as much in this age, and in the age to come eternal life."

One hundredfold (or in Luke, "many times")! Now, in this time! So, there's a lot more that will be coming our way, to God's glory, because we left a lot in those years for Him, and He has already restored everything that we gave up and way more. I'll explain more of that later. Not that we do this for the return on investment—you can't! Our heart is we give and gave Jesus everything when we surrendered to Him (He owns everything anyway, and we only have anything because He gave it to us to *manage*), so to leave a house or a property or a lucrative job (I did okay as an electrical engineer and territory technical sales manager) because He called us to can only come from the heart and is based only on faith and is done only to bring Him glory.

Even the hundredfold return will bring Him glory because it will partly be used to further His kingdom. As believers, that's just what we do!

Now, I didn't make that high salary in 2003, nor in 2004 (nor for the full twelve-year financial faith walk), but then boom! God did a new thing. I'll tell you about that later. First, I have to get you beyond 2003.

Two of the people who joined Alpha Fiber in 2003 were Christians with different skill sets and different faith walks. In fact, these two seemed to be at the two extremes. Dan wanted to be entirely led by the Spirit; he fasted so much before a meeting that he was shaking and didn't really communicate well to the president of a company. We were attempting to partner with this company, so that was a bummer; I didn't hear a call to go that far, but I had to just trust God. The other brother was so focused on getting the job done that he'd want to quickly pray and then have every item planned out in such detail that there was no room or need for faith.

That's when I knew this was going to be harder than I thought because it involved people! We are so easily moved by our emotions, our sensitivities, and our previous hurts. And we also have an enemy, the devil, who may be right around the corner, waiting for us to give him an opening that allows him to wrap our feet in duct tape (my analogy, of course).

Soon, Dan resigned from Alpha Fiber, seemingly setting us back again. Many people came and went, some for a long time, some for a short time. One young man came and said he would help with sales, pure commission; he felt the call of God to it. That afternoon he called me back and said he thought a higher commission was more appropriate, so I said okay. Two days later, he called and said I should take out a loan and pay him a base salary. That was not what we had agreed to at all, so he left before he even started. People! How does God put up with us?

Parts of our vision called for things that were ministry focused. I asked our good friend Nicole Kerr for help; I needed a good Christian corporate attorney (good at both), and she suggested one. I talked to Harris about all the parts of the vision, and he counseled me with the obvious: the ministry parts of the vision needed to be in a separate ministry. "Your for-profit company has a fiduciary responsibility to focus on profit," he said. "Any investors in the for-profit company will need to know that your goal is profit."

In February of 2004, I also talked to an accountant friend Jim about parts of the mission and vision that I felt the Lord continued to point to that were ministry focused and the parts that were for-profit focused. He suggested the same obvious conclusion: separate the two. So, after much prayer, in 2004, I also started Alpha World Ministries to focus on those ministry parts.

Though it seemed like a lot, I just wanted to continue to be obedient to what God was mapping out for me. And God always took care of us. As I mentioned, for the first three and a half years, I didn't make a penny. But after that, I didn't suddenly make a ton of money. I think I made $7,000 for the year in the fourth year. But no matter what percentage of our needs I made, God always supplied the missing percentage: whether it was the full 100 percent that He provided at first, the 90 percent, or later, the 35 percent, He always came through. God is faithful!

And God used that to minister to people too. One day He called me to talk to a guy on a corner with a sign saying he was hungry. I normally would buy them food so as not to enable them to keep an addiction going. When I talked to him about God providing, he looked me up and down, noticing my clothes were professional looking. He said, "What do you know about needing money?" "Well," I said, "I guarantee you made more money on this corner than I made all year!" I told him I made zero all year and last year too. He said, "Then how'd you get them nice shoes?" I said, "My wife just bought these at the Salvation Army store for three bucks!" Beckie is awesome like that. She finds deals and knows when to buy them. That was a brand-new-looking $90 pair of shoes that she got for $3. At that point, I had some credibility to talk to this homeless guy about God's provisions by our faith.

Even though we sometimes got food from the food bank and sometimes got clothes from the Salvation Army store or Goodwill, we knew the Lord would totally make up for anything we gave up to serve Him. And, as I mentioned, He did. After moving to Oregon and renting our Florida house, we purchased another house in Oregon since some of the other house bills were being paid by the rental income. We bought a small home in Oregon and saved some of our money, as I was feeling the Lord direct me that way. As we saved the money, the Lord sometimes whispered where to invest it and what to look into. I did some research and checked some things, but God was usually the instigator of the research and the prompting of what to do and when in those times that I heard Him.

He blessed us and continues to bless us toward His hundredfold promise. We had good gains during the next few years, and then He turned the flood in our Florida house into good with the rebuilding of the damaged house. Now it was remodeled and new looking, and the market is selling houses at much higher prices in this current seller's market. We also found another house to switch into, at a good discount, as I mentioned, because we prayed. In addition, the Lord said to diversify and invest more, and He pointed to some property that has good timber on it. Suddenly we have three houses and a timber investment, and God's not done yet. I feel the Lord is saying to take my almost forty years of technology and business experience, with many startup companies that I founded (at His prompting) and many startups that I got involved with in my career, and put it to use by investing in startup companies. Stay tuned for more on that in years to come! So, while I previously had to shop at Goodwill for shoes, and it gave me the credibility to minister to homeless people, now we're investing in Christian entrepreneurs who have solid business plans and who will run their businesses with Christian principles so that we can minister to others.

The Lord also had me stop to talk to many other homeless people during that season, and I thought my policy would be the same: never cash but food if they say they need food. I didn't want them to buy beer or drugs with it if they had an addiction. I did a rough guesstimate at the Cold Night shelter and some other ministries where I volunteered, and there seemed to be a lot of addiction and/or mental illness in the homeless there. I thought I would never give out cash. But God seems to test our conclusions against obedience and trust that He knows better. In Isaiah 55:9, God says, "As the heavens are higher than the earth, so are my ways higher than your ways and my thoughts than your thoughts."

One day I stopped to buy a guy on the corner a sandwich, and I realized this guy didn't look as frail and worn as some of the others. In fact, he looked kind of hardened and strong, totally sober, and not at all confused like some. I asked him his story, why he was homeless, and he said he had just gotten out of prison. I swallowed hard and asked him what he was in for, and he said, "Assault." I prayed! After we talked a bit, I asked him who he would most like to see in heaven. His hardened countenance changed, and he looked up a bit toward the back ceiling of the place as if looking at a person there and said, "My grandmother. She was a good lady."

I drove him down the road since I needed to get to my first meeting, and he asked to be dropped off a block away from the 7-Eleven. I asked him why a block away, and he said he needed someone to buy him some wine. He said, "You try sleeping in the woods with all the mosquitos and ants and see if you don't need something to knock you out!" I asked him why they wouldn't sell to him directly, and he said it was because they knew he was sleeping behind their building in the woods and maybe they didn't want to encourage it. I could feel the Lord nudge me to buy the guy some wine, so I did. So much for not giving cash to avoid alcohol: I just flat out bought him the alcohol! Well, I was just trying to run my race.

Speaking of running the race mapped out for you (Hebrews 12:1): *my race is not your race, and my calling is not your calling.* Gary and Fran Antonellis have a very different calling than we do, but our lives intersected on day one, and we have been blessed to call them dear friends, and brother and sister in Christ, ever since. Their calling is much different but extremely important. They open their home and their hearts and their everything to help people, refresh people, encourage people, and they consistently serve the body of Christ at the local church and in helping others. They opened their hearts and their home to foster many children, and they adopted three of them, even while some of them are yet to honor them greatly. But not one ounce of their labors of love is missed by God! First Corinthians 15:58 says:

Therefore, my dear brothers and sisters, stand firm. Let nothing move you. Always give yourselves fully to the work of the Lord, because you know that your labor in the Lord is not in vain.

And they had been throwing a party every year on Memorial Day for the local body of Christ community for twenty-five years, letting us get refreshed while swimming and jet skiing on their lake and eating and sitting and chatting and sunning ourselves. And they also had a small group in their home and faithfully served, for decades, at the church. It would take a whole book just to list the serving and the fixing and the fostering they've served God with over the years.

When we left our house for a ministry, they even let us sleep in their driveway, in our RV, since the Lord did not provide any other location for us. And they're still blessing people today, even when they don't really have room! Today they have a young woman living with them who is now thriving because of their love and support and opening of their heart and their home to her.

The point is: run the race mapped out for you, not the one mapped out for my wife and me, nor the one mapped out for Gary and Fran.

Other faithful believers who I know personally, who have also encouraged me so much, are faithfully running their race with perseverance, for years and years and years too.

Herb Lange has been serving God faithfully for over fifty years, coming back from retirement as a pastor every time a pastor was needed. He was at our church for over sixteen years the first time. I think he's come back from retirement three different times to help out three different churches. Some of his stories are amazing.

Dr. Joe John stayed as an associate pastor, even though he has a PhD in theology and easily could have been a senior pastor somewhere. He was at our church for over fifteen years, and in his retirement, he too came back to take over the leadership of Campsite Ministries in obedience to the Lord's prompting. God has done some amazing things—I mean amazing—in and through Pastor Joe and his wife Arlene's life and faithful service. I asked him if I could share some briefly (it would take two books to list what God has done through them!), and he said, "Of course."

DR. JOE JOHN

Dr. Joe John got his master's and doctorate degrees in theology and served the Lord initially as a troubleshooter and rescuer of failing churches. In his very first ministry, he was sent to Idaho to a church that was down to fifteen people. A meeting for all the districts had him fly to Fort Wayne, Indiana. His parents lived somewhat close by, so he surprised them with a visit to Bovard, Pennsylvania, about six hours away by car. His dad told him about a local friend, Johnny Melago, who was dying. Both kidneys were bad, one was removed, and his liver was also going. His dad suggested he go pray with him.

Pastor Joe talked with Mr. and Mrs. Melago and then felt he should ask him two important questions. He said, "Do you believe the Lord can heal?" "Yes," Mr. Melago answered him. Then Pastor Joe asked him, "Do you believe the Lord will heal you now?" Mr. Melago stared at him for a little while and then said, "For some reason, I do." "Then we will pray for and receive that healing," Pastor Joe said, and they did.

Since he had to get back to Idaho, Pastor Joe had to leave. His dad called him about a week later and said, "Mr. Melago keeps getting better and better, ever since you prayed with him!" And then they found out that even though one of Mr. Melago's kidneys was removed and the other was bad, he now somehow had two good kidneys, and his liver was also healed. God had healed and restored him!

Another miracle was when Pastor Joe was pastoring a church in Pomona, California. He was driving, and a guy dressed in white was walking. Pastor Joe felt the Lord say, "Stop and pick him up." He didn't think it was safe, but the voice got stronger. So even though he had passed him slightly, Pastor Joe pulled over, and this guy in white got in the back seat. He said he was just going up the road and the Master wanted Pastor Joe to preach on a few key scriptures that coming Sunday. He said if Pastor Joe was obedient and preached on those scriptures, there would be healings in his church on Sunday morning. Pastor Joe said he let the guy off by the exit, and then he couldn't see the guy at all anymore. He was just gone!

That Sunday, he preached on the scriptures the guy in white instructed him to preach on. A woman who had bad skin cancer was going to go on Monday to have students view the sores she had on her skin. Nothing was working in her cancer treatments, so she had a lot of sores. It was a difficult cancer to treat and a bit rare, so she agreed to let this group of students learn and take pictures of her skin sores. During the service, Pastor Joe called for people to come up if they needed prayer for healing. This woman came up, and Pastor Joe laid his hands on her and prayed for her. As he did, he felt "something go out," he said. Pastor Joe's secretary also came up for healing. Pastor Joe laid hands on her and prayed because she had one eye that went to the right. He felt something go out while he prayed for her too. Nothing looked different in either one of them immediately that Sunday morning, but Pastor Joe told them all to thank God for their healings. His secretary told him that night when she thanked God for her healing, her eye immediately straightened! The woman with the skin cancer and sores had no sores on her skin the next day when the students were viewing her skin. She told them she was healed in church the previous day! She hadn't even received salvation in Jesus yet, but she came back the next Sunday and did.

Pastor Joe told me, "We've seen others too. It's about faith and obedience, God told me. I think anybody can pray that way. In the hospital, I've had God tell me, 'I'm going to heal this one today.' I tell them to believe and to say it out loud." Pastor Joe continued, "One guy needed a heart transplant. He sang in the choir, and we prayed over him. He no longer needed a heart transplant. I've seen people healed of cancer. One person was healed over the phone! You just can't put God in a box and say He will or won't do anything. He can do all things! There were other times where I would pray, and I wouldn't hear anything, just silence. And still other times I would hear God whisper, 'That's not My will.'"

I'm sure Pastor Joe has dozens and dozens of stories of God moving in and through him and his wife, Arlene, as they faithfully served Him for over fifty years and continue to serve Him, even into their seventies.

My favorite story with Pastor Joe, though, is this next one:

In 2009 and 2010, Pastor Joe was going through serious medical troubles with his liver. He had last-stage nonalcoholic cirrhosis of the liver, and he had cancer on his liver and his pancreas. The doctor told him he had about three to four months to live. He was getting weaker and weaker; his teeth were getting weaker; his fingernails were falling out, and he had his teeth pulled. I remember the prayer requests coming out about Pastor Joe.

"Doctors wanted to know, since I never drank alcohol, how I got this," he said. They wanted to take pieces of his liver and biopsy them and study them. It's extremely rare to get a nonalcoholic liver problem like this. Pastor Joe and Arlene said okay to the biopsy and study. The doctor said his liver was getting to be very brittle and there was a real possibility that he could bleed out. Pastor Joe said, "I'm okay to go if the Lord wants me to go." And the doctor set the biopsy up for the following Monday at the community hospital in New Port Richey.

Even though he was pretty weak, on Sunday, June 13, 2010, he went to pick up their granddaughter Hope from the youth group. He feebly walked in and leaned against the back wall. Pastor Joe recalled, "Kids were in groups praying, and three boys came up to me and asked if I was Hope's grandfather. 'She said you might die tomorrow?' I said, 'Yes, there's a procedure, and there's a chance I could bleed out.' We held hands, and they began to pray. The oldest boy led in prayer. I felt like hot oil went throughout my body. The boys jumped and asked, 'What was that?' and I said, 'I believe your prayer was answered.' I started feeling strength coming back right away."

Then some girls came over with Hope and asked to pray. They started to pray, and one girl said, "I can't pray. I just hear you're healed and shouldn't worry about it." Pastor Joe told them the Lord just brought healing through the prayers and thanked them.

Pastor Joe continued, "The next day, on June 14, 2010, I had the biopsy. A specialist from Jacksonville was brought in to do it. They had a team ready to do something if I started to bleed out. They took me in and put the X-ray or whatever on me. The specialist said to me, 'Um, your liver is supposed to be three times its normal size, right?' and I said yes. He said, 'Hm.' I said, 'It isn't?' He said, 'No, it isn't.'

"He went in and took three pieces of the liver, from different sections inside and the far edge. Then he said, 'Okay, we're done.' I said, 'I didn't bleed out?' He said, 'No, that's strange.' He looked at the X-rays and said, 'You're the same person in both X-rays, right?' I was the only one they did for that test in that hospital that day.

"I went home. My doctor was on vacation, so we went to the hospital exactly two weeks later, on June 28. The doctor lifted my case file in the air, dropped it on the desk, and said, 'You have a new pink young man's liver in you, and we can't figure it out!' And my pancreas was healed too! The Lord healed me on the spot when the youth prayed for me! I was able to do all sorts of things, and my strength was back."

That was ten years ago. Wow, God is so good! From potentially bleeding out during a test or dying in three to four months to being miraculously healed on the spot with a pink new liver and healthy pancreas!

Other men of faith running their race with perseverance: Ray Owens started out as a youth minister and never stopped ministering to create leaders of leaders who are still ministering to this day through his Family Discipleship Ministries (FDM). Many people have grown in faith and in the Word out of what God has done through Ray, including Eddie and Beth Taylor, now with Taylor Ministry Group. One day at a youth retreat, Eddie Taylor gave a message called, "Get Messy." Loving other people can get messy, but God calls us to it, and it's worth it: both will be blessed (that's my super short paraphrase). Eddie was talking to the youth, but I've never forgotten it. And I've gotten a little messy, by God's grace; anything good in me is from heaven. I'm just a turkey, but for some reason, God calls me and you to soar like eagles in His name and with His power and with His love. And we could if we trust Him.

I talked to Nicole Kerr, who was a teenager in the youth group. She said Ray really taught them how to worship. They would sometimes go in the sanctuary on Sunday night and sit on the floor and pray and sing and just let God meet with them. It was so powerful and fantastic that as teenage kids, they'd rather be there and do that than anything else. Plus, it was a tight-knit group of believers being there for each other and studying the Word together.

She said one evening during worship, she and Paula Whitaker went outside, and both had the same vision. Paula recalled telling the small group left inside that she had a vision of a map, with light shining out from Tarpon Springs outward. Nicole said she received the same vision! They felt that God was saying He would be sending His light and His love out from this place to many other places. This was before Nicole's sister Ariadne went to Russia to minister and help orphaned babies, and this was before Eddie Taylor went out, and many, many others. God did indeed send many people out from Tarpon!

And Jimmy Smuda, senior pastor of Trinity Assembly of God, whose love for people is just absolutely relentless, including his joy and energy and love for his wife and children, that makes me want to be a better husband and father just watching him.

Missionaries who have been serving globally for decades (whose names I'll omit for protection) at great cost. Great cost to themselves! They have a great impact in many locations. I don't put myself in the same category as any of these people, just that I'm trying to run my race with perseverance. You should run yours too.

And many, many more people who are faithfully running with perseverance the race mapped out for them, driven by this love of God that makes us whole. They are all an inspiration to me. Do you have that list of faithful people you are learning under and getting encouraged and inspired by?

Are you studying the Bible and listening to leaders who God has faithfully used for decades? We have done a lot of Bible studies in our home with our small groups, and one of our favorites is the Jim Cymbala study called "When God's people pray." Jim Cymbala is pastor of the

Brooklyn Tabernacle Church. I highly recommend the video-driven study. We also found the message he talks about in the study fantastic! Or lately, we did Louie Giglio, pastor of Passion City Church, study on the book of Colossians. We also love his Passion Conferences. And we also did the book of James with Matt Chandler, another good one. The point is: there are great teachers out there who have been faithfully preaching solid biblical principles from the Word for decades. Note the key words here: "solid," "biblical," and "from the Word." Anything that deviates from the living Word you should run from.

Speaking of deviating from the living Word, I would be totally negligent if I didn't address the current issues of the day here at the end of 2021. We've just come from a horrendous two years of COVID-19 problems and stresses, and we have cultural, political, economic, and social fallout all over. We previously had the worst attack via politics that I've ever seen in my whole life, and I've been voting for forty years. The globe is now divided into two camps, setting the stage for end-time events according to the Bible like never before. And there is so much deception it is hard to fathom that some people fall for the fake social-media accounts intended to portray much more volume for an issue than is really there, and the polarized news-media stories doing the same. The deception is tremendous.

But we have the Word of God to address all issues, so we cannot be lied to successfully. So, I have to unemotionally address some of the most important issues of today that are buried in deceit and leading to tremendous pain and suffering.

Life versus Abortion. We now know that God cares about all life, from the moment of conception until natural death, because He says He is the one who forms life in the womb. He cares about babies in the womb (Jeremiah 1:5). And we are all fearfully and wonderfully made by Him (Psalm 139:14). And every day of our life has been written in His book before even one of them came to pass (meaning before we are even born). It is clear God cares about the infant in the womb and already has plans for her or him.

It is really sad that this has become a political discussion, but with the latest technology in 3D ultrasound, we can now see just how human that little guy or gal is. His or her heart is beating at about eight weeks into the pregnancy. Early on, we didn't know, but now we can see clearly. This is the biggest tragedy of our century, and it is the saddest because it is avoidable if we just live our lives in God's loving way.

Purity until Marriage versus Sexual Immorality. God calls all sex outside of the marriage of one man with one woman sin, not His design for the beautiful life. This includes homosexuality, heterosexual sex before marriage, sex with someone who is not your spouse, sex with your boyfriend or girlfriend even if you love them, all of it.

First Thessalonians 4:3 says, "It is God's will that you should be sanctified: that you should avoid sexual immorality."

Hebrews 13:4 says, "Marriage should be honored by all, and the marriage bed kept pure, for God will judge the adulterer and all the sexually immoral."

Romans 1:21–28 says,

For although they knew God, they neither glorified him as God nor gave thanks to him, but their thinking became futile and their foolish hearts were darkened. Although they claimed to be wise, they became fools and exchanged the glory of the immortal God for images made to look like a mortal human being and birds and animals and reptiles.

Therefore God gave them over in the sinful desires of their hearts to sexual impurity for the degrading of their bodies with one another. They exchanged the truth about God for a lie, and worshiped and served created things rather than the Creator—who is forever praised. Amen.

Because of this, God gave them over to shameful lusts. Even their women exchanged natural sexual relations for unnatural ones. In the same way the men also abandoned natural relations with women and were inflamed with lust for one another. Men committed shameful acts with other men, and received in themselves the due penalty for their error. Furthermore, just as they did not think it worthwhile to retain the knowledge of God, so God gave them over to a depraved mind, so that they do what ought not to be done.

Now, this is not me condemning in any way, but this is God's Word highlighting two things: He loves you and sin is not okay. That's God's message for all of our sins: He loves you and sin is not okay. Do you understand both of those things go together? The living God loves you, as is, no conditions, while you're still having the wrong kind of sex, while you're still being selfish, while you're being cruel. It's important to know that love. But it is also important to know that it is not okay to keep doing those things that God says not to do. They lead to death in the end. They keep you from the joyful, loving, abundant life that Jesus came to give us. And His part is finished, so this joyful, loving, abundant life is readily available to all of us. Just reach out and receive Jesus by faith, begin to live it, and enjoy it. It is here for you now.

But for some reason, some in the culture have gone beyond sex outside of marriage and same-sex attraction to gender confusion. This used to be considered a mental illness by the experts. Now some groups are trying to sell the world that a person isn't just male or female! That in-between or flip-flopping is okay. That's insane and obviously incorrect. Can you believe we even have to address this? Just look at the two different creations, both wonderfully made but very different. Genesis 1:27 says, "So God created mankind in his own image, in the image of God he created them; male and female he created them."

Genesis 5:1–2 says, "When God created mankind, he made them in the likeness of God. He created them male and female and blessed them."

It seems just so crazy that we have to talk about this. Are people actually trying to say that a boy is not a boy and a girl is not a girl? I don't even know what to say. Would you even reject the obvious just to reject God?

What is really scary is verse 28 above in Romans 1. If people don't stop rejecting God, they run the risk of verse 28: God gives them over to a depraved mind. I think that is what is driving some of the insanity. Oh yes, there is a political agenda that some are seeking. But people believing it? That's a mind that refuses to even look at the obvious. A boy with his male organs can be considered a girl? That's nuts!

And beyond trying to erase the previous version of the American Psychiatric Associations' classification of gender confusion as a mental illness, they now want to disallow young people who want help from getting help. That's child abuse, and that's evil. Preventing the child who wants to get help from getting help? In the category of highest suicide rate? That's evil!

When we get to that level of obvious evil, we know there is more than just politics involved. This is a big push of spiritual darkness, along with all sorts of deception. Once again: there are political agendas behind some of the division, but there are alliances pulling together that are normally quite opposed to each other. This means we need to pray. This is a spiritual battle, and we are not opposed to people. We are opposed to the spiritual forces of the devil who promotes evil and the destruction of people's lives. We, instead, love people and pray. We pray against the devil's lies, and we love all people. I'm going to say that a third time because I know how hard it is: we pray against the devil's lies, and we love all people. Of course, we also act. We also vote and rally others to vote based on our biblical values and the scriptures that back them up to hold our leaders accountable. But what moves the needle is when we pray.

As we pray, God is responding with our eyes being opened, love breaking through, and people coming to Christ. There appears to be quite a drive to divide people. There's division over how to deal with the COVID-19 virus, the masks, the vaccines, people's privacy, and people's rights globally. It seems as though some people have plans to just lie and present their cause as good. Some people are pushing for socialist and communist ideals in America, but we know from the Word of God that a fallen humanity cannot be trusted to have all that control without accountability. Our present democratic republic instills accountability.

I think many more young people today believe socialism is good because they think they will get a free iPhone or get other free things that they didn't earn, and the political agendas promote that as normal. But what always ends up happening is everyone gets the equivalent of free bread after they wait in long bread lines because the leadership with full control wants more steak and wine!

So, they lie and call it good, but one only has to look at fascism in Nazi Germany, communism in Russia or China, socialism in Cuba or Venezuela to get a real look at how that totalitarian government control turns out for people. Ask any of the immigrants fleeing those countries how good it was to have everything shared. And some of these drastic lies are causing people to stumble, and Jesus said, "Woe to the person through whom they come," in Matthew 18:7. If you're pushing fake agendas that are hurting people, you will be in deep trouble with the Lord of the universe if you don't stop it and turn around.

But there is good news for anyone. Any and all of our wickedness can and will be forgiven and removed forever by us just asking for God's free gift of forgiveness! All you have to do is look and believe. Your entire list of dumb things and sins and everything will be wiped clean, white as snow. And you will, instead, get Jesus's list of great things as though they are your list (His righteousness is given to us). Forevermore, when God the Father looks at you, He will see His Son, Jesus, in terms of your deeds. Do you understand how amazingly great that is? You and I get to go from dirty, with a terrible judgment awaiting us, to clean as can be, with an awesome eternity awaiting us!

Jesus said there would be all sorts of false teachers and all sorts of deception as we get closer to the "game over." If you're reading this next week or after I've left the earth (from either the rapture or end of my days), please read all of your Bible quickly, for yourself, so you will not be deceived.

KEEP GOING

There were so many things I could sense God was doing, and there were so many things that He called my family and me to walk through. In January of the year before starting the company, which is January 2002, Pastor Lange asked me to take over the chair of the church council. We had also just implemented small groups in our church, and my wife and I started a small group that God just blessed! That became such a wonderful small group, and it grew so large that we had to split into two smaller groups. None of us wanted to split, but it was the right thing to do so others could experience that deep family that was developing. We had twenty-eight adults that split into two groups of fourteen. We are still close after all these years, and some of them just came over this year, nineteen years later, in 2021, to start yet another small group!

If you're not in a small group, as a believer in Christ, get in one right away. There's no better way to walk this Christian life than do it together with other Christians. It is the best way to live this Christian life!

You know, I continue to take notes on what God is doing almost daily because I fully expect many more miracles to take place in my life and the lives of all believers. That's what God said in His Word. He guarantees it, so I guarantee it and believe it.

In 2021, I think we are already seeing a move of God across the planet as we've never seen before. There is such a global division going on right now, and at the same time, a global move of God is going on. I want to be a part of what He's doing and not just watching it, just as Pastor Aaron said in his July 6 prayer!

And it continues to amaze me that the God of the universe pays attention to me! I am literally sitting here by myself, back in Florida. After we drove the trailer back to Oregon, driving 3,400 miles, with nine stops, across eleven days (we don't go more than five or so hours per day with a special-needs girl), I took a week in Oregon and then flew back to Florida to babysit the contractors.

Even before the pandemic, there seemed to be a lot of people who didn't complete their jobs. I've been calling it an epidemic of incompetence, or maybe I should be saying, incompleteness. People seem to be doing 80 percent to 90 percent of what they're supposed to be doing, and they're satisfied with that. They're almost surprised when I'm not!

Of course, now, with all of the extra payments workers have received from the Federal Government for COVID-19 relief, many have felt they don't need to return to work, so there is a tremendous shortage of workers across the nation. There are help-wanted signs everywhere, and restaurants and all sorts of service-related businesses, like auto repair and such, are quoting much longer wait times because they are short-staffed. I wonder what new cultural environment this will create that the Lord will use to draw people to Himself. We should be ready to give a reason for the hope that is in us with respect and gentleness (1 Peter 3:15).

But as I sat there by myself, checking off all the tasks required to complete the repairs on the house, I was praying (again) to get closer to God! I'm realizing (again) that nothing else can do what knowing God can do.

I'm not talking about just believing there is some sort of a god; I'm talking about knowing the real, living God, hanging out with Him, hearing from Him, and sensing this encouragement that just lifts your soul. Nothing else can do that! I want more of that, so I want to know Him more. I can hear that late '90s SonicFlood's song "I want to see your face; I want to know you more." I'm singing that to myself: I want to know you more, Lord!

As I sit here honestly asking my God to grant that, I'm nudged to the bookshelf, where an old Beth Moore Bible study of my wife is sitting, *Jesus, The One and Only.* I grab it since the Holy Spirit is nudging me there and it seems like it might begin to answer my prayer. Here's part of what I read in the intro from Beth Moore:

I can echo a hint of the emotion Paul felt when he claimed, "I am jealous for you with a godly jealousy" (2 Corinthians 11:2). I want more of the abundance of Christ for you. No matter how much you have. More! I want you to be jealous for me to have His increasing abundance, too. I'm jealous for us to want Him more than we want blessing, health, or even breath. I want to know Him so well that my undivided heart can exclaim, "Because Your love is better than life, my lips will glorify You" (Psalm 63:3). Better than life![5]

Wow, no matter where I am, no matter what I'm thinking, the Lord is always here with me and always paying attention. That amazes me!

Miracle 80. Today, Jesus reaches out in answer to my prayer to know Him more by pointing me to an old Bible study that is focused on knowing Him more just to say to me, "I'm right here, Rich. I'm still right here."

I shouldn't be amazed since God says it in His Word, but I am. King David was amazed too. He said, in Psalm 8:4–9:

What is mankind that you are mindful of them, human beings that you care for them?

You have made them a little lower than the angels and crowned them with glory and honor. You made them rulers over the works of your hands; you put everything under their feet: all flocks and herds, and the animals of the wild, the birds in the sky, and the fish in the sea, all that swim the paths of the seas. Lord, our Lord, how majestic is your name in all the earth!

I continue to sense God nudging me forward, and I continue to hear His voice.

Let us go back to those next years now, where I tried to create the company God wanted me to create and the ministry God wanted me to create. I tried to find the provisions that God was providing, and we changed the company's focus a few times. We got approval to be a competitive phone company (ALEC: Alternative Local Exchange

[5] Beth Moore, *Jesus the One and Only* (Nashville: Lifeway Christian Resources, 2000), 6.

Carrier) at that time, so we tried to resell phone service and DSL data service while bidding on fiber-to-the-home projects. We met with other business leaders, other Christians, potential partners, potential employees, hired people, etc.

We thought we might hook churches together for greater impact; we identified five different types of connections to our potential network with various partners, and we sought the best broadband-access technology (which communications service providers continue to seek today, of course).

Two people who came to help me, even though we had no money, included Juanita, who helped me tremendously by doing some administrative tasks, and Frank Del Percio, who helped a lot by trying to sell the services we were lining up. They also helped spiritually by praying with us and for Beckie and me, and they helped emotionally by just being there and being our friends.

One afternoon around noon, I asked Frank to help me with something, and he said, "Not now, it's a beautiful day out there, and I'll be out there for lunch! Don't you ever enjoy your waterfront?" I stopped and watched him open the sliding glass door, step out onto the patio, and turn around to call me outside. "Come on; this is God's beauty. Enjoy it!" So, I did! I realized that I was getting so focused on trying to get something started that I wasn't even resting and enjoying this beauty that was right in front of me. Thank you, Frank, for the reminder!

With Pastor Ken Zimmerman as our new pastor (Pastor Herb retired for the first of three or four times, so far), I went to him for prayer and advice. He suggested I consider carefully what burdens the family would be under with small children at home. Pastor Ken was great. He used to help keep everyone grounded by reminding us to "keep the main thing, the main thing!" In other words, keep the good news of Jesus as the main thing that we are always about. Let that guide decision-making, relationships with people, and the planning in the church (I was chair of the administrative council), in our home life, and working at our jobs.

As I was expressing my worries about everything to Pastor Ken during one of our Wednesday night basketball evenings at the church—another thing I loved about Pastor Ken—I was hoping for an easy button. Instead, Pastor Ken suggested I read two books. This was the last thing I wanted to hear. A book? Really? He suggested *Visioneering* by Andy Stanley, which counsels us to use the book of Nehemiah as a guide for what to do when God gives you a vision—a good book! And he also suggested George Müller, who miraculously took care of thousands of orphans, starting in 1834 in England, by just praying. Müller never asked for funds, ever, but always and only prayed about all needs. His intention was to prove that prayer works, and boy, did he! He built buildings and took care of over 10,000 orphans during his lifetime by always just praying. People would just bring to him what God put on their hearts to bring!

I have to tell you: I did not want this answer from Pastor Ken; I wanted easy. My wife and I were trying to raise our three children, one of whom is a special-needs girl who requires a lot of extra effort. And the pressure of all that plus not having money coming in weighed on us heavily at times. I wanted something easy. But nevertheless, I read the books because I felt that God would advise me through His Word, through His Holy Spirit, through prayers, and through the pastor He brought in to help shepherd our lives.

Pastor Ken also practiced what he preached, literally. He felt God call him to build bridges to the rest of the Tarpon Springs community, so he undertook to pull together a National Day of Prayer event. I really felt called to this unity part, so I helped. Pastor Ken and a ton of other pastors, lay leaders, and volunteers pulled together in May of 2004, a National Day of Prayer event that brought fourteen different churches together to pray, with over 500 people in attendance in the Tarpon Springs High School stadium. No other names were mentioned, no names of churches or organizations, just the name of Jesus! That's the way Pastor Ken said it needed to be from the start: keeping the main thing, the main thing!

While I was getting some work done on some drywall in our house, I struck up a conversation about God with the guy doing the work. He said his biggest questions currently were the real roles that he should be focused on as a husband and as a father. God continued to point me toward teachings and content that Alpha World Ministries could bring out to help people like Him. So, I prayed, with the faith of George Müller, that God would continue to just bring whatever was needed.

God moved someone's heart, and this person brought $5,000 for Alpha World Ministries. Just like that! She insisted, said she had to. Boom, *miracle 81*!

Three years later, in 2007, as we planned out the first Do You Believe event (more on that soon), we needed money for the TV ad. A woman rang my front doorbell. When I answered, she handed me a check for $2,000 for the ministry and said, "I wrestled with God for three nights before bringing this check. Don't ask," she said. *Miracle 82*!

Back to 2004: on the business side, we met other people who had a similar calling from heaven, a telecom technology for Jesus! In November of 2004, one of the fiber-equipment vendors asked me if I wanted to meet another lunatic doing the same fiber-for-Jesus startup in Atlanta. He said they had already installed his equipment in a headend and a bunch of fiber and were providing data, voice, and video to customers. Of course, I did and said so!

After praying about it and feeling like it was God's will but not understanding it ("lean not on your own understanding"), I took my last $500 and flew to Atlanta. I met with the people who had founded Qlevr Media. Great people! Brian and his wife let me stay in their small place for the night. They had no room, but they were kind enough to just stretch out an air mattress on the floor. All the Qlevr people were awesome brothers and sisters in Christ. It was like we were family without even knowing each other.

They told me about their initial ministry to the poor in Atlanta and how God just used them to minister to hurting people. It was awesome to hear, but I kept wondering why I was there. I expected to find a thriving business, but as it turned out, they lost their main investor. I prayed with and for them, and they prayed with and for me. I also met some people from a ministry called Reasons to Believe. These were deep technical scientists showing that the solid reasons to believe in Jesus extend into even the deep technical details in every area of science: astronomy, biology, geology, etc.

I headed back to the Atlanta airport in a taxi, though, wondering why I had been there. Nothing had really gotten done that was substantial, right? Was it just to pray with them, or did God have more things in mind? I wondered if I was even really hearing from God (honestly). We see through a glass dimly lit, but what if I'm not even looking in the right glass? What if it's all just from too much pizza before bed?

In my mind, I went through all the reasons why I must be an idiot: I had a wife and three little kids that were depending on me and no real job. I didn't make any money! And I had just spent my last $500, only to find out they might go out of business. People had come and left the company; we were not making progress here! I had been at this for two whole years. Do you know how many things have to fall into place for anything substantive to happen here? *Maybe I should just stop being an idiot and go get a real job*, I thought.

In the one or two paragraphs that I used to describe the two-year journey to this point, that barely scratches the surface of what that took on a day-to-day basis. Just from the business perspective, that meant selling computers and printers and software to businesses and consumers. It meant creating the processes to buy them from suppliers and distributors, have returns/warranty processes, hire technicians (most of the work I did myself) while still writing and editing a larger fiber-to-the-home business plan, examining fiber technologies, etc., etc., etc.

Now imagine someone's home life with this going on:

"Hi, honey, I had a good day pounding my head against all sorts of technical things and business things while you're taking care of three little kids, and don't worry: things are going great!"

Wife: "Oh, that's great. Did we make any money yet?"

Husband: "No, not yet, but don't worry: God will provide!"

Wife: "How long are you going to keep saying that baloney to me? It's been two years."

Husband: "Honey, put down the frying pan."

That's an imaginary story in case you need another cup of coffee today. My wife, Beckie, was fantastic but not immune. You have to realize that she wasn't given the vision! She didn't write down the outline; she didn't feel the calling. She supported me like Sarah supported Abraham. "Get up and go," God told Abraham but not Sarah. She had to trust that he heard correctly all along the way. That's pretty hard! So, I thank Beckie for her trust, her support, her patience when I got it wrong, her prayers, her love. I'm so blessed to have her by my side, with the spirit that God put and molded in her.

I could almost cry in the taxi ride back to the Atlanta airport, but real men don't do that, so I didn't (I grew up on Clint Eastwood). But God (there it is again: the Gospel in two words), in His mercy and His grace, sent a messenger. I noticed a book with gold edges sitting on the center console in the front of the SUV. I said, "Is that your Bible?" I was really just making small talk; I wasn't really in the mood to say any more than that. No sermon was on the way, if you know what I mean. No Sunday school lesson was I prepared to bring out; I was in no shape to tell anyone anything: my strength was pretty low, and I was starting to get pretty scared that I would fail miserably. I could see the huge size of the storm and how small my little rowboat was out in the middle of the ocean, without oars. And everyone knows what happens in a huge storm if you're in a tiny boat: boats sink, and people die.

The driver nearly jumped out of his seat when I said, "Is that your Bible?" and he said, "Wow, okay. You're the one! Okay, here." And he handed me the Bible while keeping his eyes on the road (thankfully!). And he said, "Open to the page with the sticky note: God said to bring that to you. I couldn't leave the house this morning without that! I don't bring my Bible out, normally."

I turned to the page with the sticky note, and it was Joshua 1:9. "Be strong and courageous" was highlighted in yellow from verse 6. In the next verse, seventh, "Be strong and very courageous" was also highlighted in yellow. And something started to rise up inside of me, as I noticed all of verse 9 was highlighted in yellow: "Have I not commanded you? Be strong and courageous. Do not be afraid; do not be discouraged, for the Lord your God will be with you wherever you go."

I almost screamed, "What? Why do you have this? Did God send you with this for me? You don't know me! How did you know I would need this?"

"You need this?" the driver almost screamed too. He was just as excited. He thought he heard from God too and was wondering if he was crazy too!

Miracle 83. God sends me a message, just in time, by prompting a taxi driver to bring his Bible with key scriptures highlighted and be prepared to give it to the passenger He identifies.

That's how it went for years! I would start to lose hope, and God would appear and confirm His leading, and my faith would be restrengthened. How could I not just keep going? I had no idea where this would end up, and I still don't, but that's the life of a believer in Jesus Christ: we walk by faith, not by sight. Oh, of course, we don't close our eyes; of course, we don't give up normal wisdom—quite the opposite. We seek wise, godly counsel.

May I stop right here and tell you something else, please? This is something God has led me to tell many, many people, including myself: as fast as you can, read the whole Bible. The Word of God is essential to living. Talk about wise counsel: the Author of life wrote the book on life. Read it; don't delay. Try not to miss a day but don't make it a chore; make sure you understand that the Giver of life loves you and wrote that for you.

That's where everything we need to navigate life starts: it's all in the Word! Read the whole thing, get the full counsel of God. When you're finished, read it again, then again, then again. You will never exhaust it of good things for you. It (or He—Jesus is the Word—read John 1:1) is loaded with good things for you.

I used to see my grandmother reading her Bible all the time. And I would say to her, "Sito," which means "grandma" in Arabic: she was born in Lebanon but had to flee Christian persecution there. I would say, "Sito, when are you going to be done reading that book?" But she never stopped reading it. Now I know why.

Listen, you can't be lied to by the enemy of your soul if you know the truth. Do you hear me? There is an enemy of your soul. He wants you all messed up in anything; he doesn't care what he uses to mess you up. But he can't lie to you in certain areas if you already know the truth in those areas. The Bible contains all the truth in all the areas. Read it as fast as you can before a lie begins (or continues) to mess you up! It will also show you how to untangle whatever was used to mess you up (freedom is available and waiting).

Back to wise counsel: there's a bunch of scriptures in the Bible that talk about seeking wise counsel. That's why I talked to every solid Christian I could about each step and each question, even when I just wanted to know why I seemed to be so far out in the air off a cliff.

Remember Neil's quote: "You can't tell that the hand of God can hold you up if He calls you to step off a cliff until you step off the cliff!" And in the Word of God is where you will find the wisdom to know if He has called you to step off a cliff. That is, of course, very important! I do *not* advocate doing stupid things and saying, "God told me to."

But likewise, if God tells you to and wise counsel confirms it and God confirms it, then walk by faith, not by fear.

One day, while trying to get service-level agreements (SLA) to resell DSL service and all sorts of other technical and business details, I tried to keep my eyes on Jesus and not freak out about paying the mortgage. I was staying confident that God had this. I was saying it out loud (that helps: confess with your mouth and believe in your heart [Romans 10:9]). When I do that, faith stays with me; it rises up inside of me.

As I balanced my checkbook with this faith, I was using my bank statements showing the checks I wrote. I caught up with balancing the checkbook after a couple of months, which was very unusual for me, but I had so many things I was trying to do. During that balancing, I found that I made a $5K mistake somehow! There was an extra $5K in my checking account. Now, if you know me, you know that's a miracle. I'm the guy who doesn't stop until he finds the missing ten cents, so there is no way that I made a mistake of that magnitude. But somehow, I did because the oil will never, ever, run out! *Miracle 84!*

We talked to a lot of people in those early years, searching for the technical and business way forward that the Lord might be making. I wondered, again, if there was a biblical precedent for what seemed to be groping in the dark, trying something here, and it doesn't work out, then trying the next thing, and it doesn't work out.

It turns out a guy named Isaac (Abraham's son, through whom God will build a mighty nation) had a similar situation. In Genesis 26:19, we read that he dug a well, but the locals in Gerar said it was their water. They dug another well, but that didn't work out all right either. They moved further away and dug a third well.

According to our business plan, we needed about 1,500 homes to hook up to fiber to break even and start making money. We approached a company called Jireh, which had a lot of development going on in the area, but they had already been making their plans for the last year. We looked at existing fiber already in the ground; we looked at municipalities and how to get to those; we looked at digging up the existing streets and sidewalks (enormously expensive, obviously!). We looked at Ariel (on poles like cable companies), and we looked at trenching.

Scott Allen Wenzel and I drove around the area, looking at fiber, looking at collocation points; we looked at how to get fiber installed while Fishel was trenching and installing for power companies. I was trying all of this while still trying to maintain and grow a computer-services business to make a dollar, while chairing the administrative council at church, hosting a small group in our home, and raising a family with a wife and three children.

So, yet again, I had to question, am I insane? Am I messing this up? I arranged to have coffee with David Bolton, an on-fire-for-Jesus

Christian man lighting up an entire youth group for Jesus at that time. This guy had it going on! *Maybe he can tell me what I'm missing here*, I thought.

I remember telling him the whole story (what a good man to listen to my whole rant; it probably took me twenty minutes straight, without taking a breath). And I asked him, almost crying again, "What if I'm messing this up? What if I'm messing up God's plan and messing up my children and my wife and my life and everything?"

And he said something I'll never forget: he said, "Rich, I don't think you're big enough to mess up God's plan. No one can stop His plans." David credits the Holy Spirit with the boldness to respond this way!

That's when I searched the Scriptures some more for that too. Do you know how many stupid things Abraham did, Isaac did, all these forefathers did? Like lying and telling kings that their wife was their sister. Did you know Abraham did that twice (Genesis 12 and 20), and his son Isaac did it too (Genesis 26)? But they couldn't stop God's plan. I bet you know Saul was going after Christians and cast his vote for their death (Acts 26:10), but he couldn't stop God's plan for him to become Paul and be a superapostle!

So, like Isaac, we "dug another well" by looking into wireless technologies (instead of wired fiber) to connect to businesses and houses. No water for us there either! But my wife and I kept going. Oh, we had to keep going at this point. But I believe we did it with faith, especially when people like David prayed for us and with us. We got scared when we took our eyes off Jesus. We got faith when we put our eyes back on Jesus, so the prayers really helped (and still do).

Paul asked for prayer in many of his letters, even while he was implementing the miraculous globally. We are to pray for each other: there's power in that. Right now, I am texting with four of my forever-family members from Intel. I'm praying that God gives them power and blesses them, that He gives them peace while He works all things for their good. And they are praying for me. That's why I'm writing in this book and not watching TV or something else.

After bidding on a 1,600 home subdivision for fiber in Polk County (remember we needed 1,500 homes to break even), we didn't get it. Phil, who was now working with Alpha Fiber, knew the chief operating officer from a previous fiber ring he helped put around Tallahassee. When we didn't get it, we asked him what else he needed. As a builder doing about 400 homes per year, they needed someone new to be their low-voltage wiring sub. So, we agreed to do it. We were both electrical engineers, with business experience also, so we could figure it out. And we did. So, suddenly we were in the construction world. We hired a team of installers and built our processes for installation, sales, billing, returns, etc.

I wondered if I was still in the center of God's will. As an electrical engineer with international-sales management experience, I was suddenly on a ladder, pulling cables. I didn't mind at all if that's what God wanted, but I wondered if He did. Was I actually being a good steward of what He has so far trained me to do and the value of that experience? So, I asked the Lord while working on a ladder, and He answered me with a young man working for an electrician as I came down the ladder! I felt led to engage him in conversation, even though we hadn't met. As it turned out, his brother died from a drug overdose, and he needed encouragement (and guidance: he was still considering doing the less dangerous illegal drugs, he said, even though his brother just died).

Miracle 85. I was there at just the right time for the Lord to provide encouragement and advice to a young man who needed it. And the Lord answered my question at the same time: that He had indeed sent me there, at this time, for people like that young man.

One day, my wife and I discussed that we needed a vacation, but I was working a lot and trying to keep many balls in the air. But we decided, by faith, God was able. So, we prayed for a vacation, and my schedule began to open up for a week. We decided that would be the week, so we began to plan for it by faith. We were still not making enough money to pay our bills, but God is faithful.

Beckie said she would like to go see the leaves change in perhaps the Smoky Mountains of North Carolina. So, we planned for that, not knowing how God would pull it off but confident that He would!

Beckie went running/walking through the next-door community, as she often did, and talked to and prayed with some of the people there. As she talked to Dee, who recently lost her husband, Bob, Beckie asked Dee what we could pray for. Dee said, "Pray for someone to take Bob's motor home and give it a long-distance run." "What?" Beckie said, "You mean like a trip to North Carolina?" And Dee said, "Oh, would you?"

Miracle 86. God opens up our schedule and gives us a class A beautiful motor home to borrow for a wonderful, much-needed vacation in the Smoky Mountains!

Alex, our oldest, had started playing acoustic guitar after trying out a few other instruments. Both of our boys really have a gift for music. One day Alex came to me and asked what he should do to get an electric guitar. He'd been saving up and had about $69, and the cheapest electrical guitar with a cheap amplifier was $99. But he really wanted the next one up that was $129: it had so much more.

I knew he was hoping I would just give him $60, but I said instead, "Let's pray. Maybe God wants to get you one even better!" I could see him exhale and put his head down a bit. "Okay," he grumbled. And we prayed.

Not long after, Dave called me and said, during one of our conversations, "Hey, is Alex still messing around with the guitar?" I said, "Yes, he's trying to buy one but not sure which one to buy." "He can have one of mine," Dave said. "I have a few of them that I can't sell, and he can just have the electric." It turned out that it was a $900 guitar when new! *Miracle 87!*

After a while, Phil suddenly left Alpha Fiber. I think he got scared. It's very hard to work for nearly nothing, by faith, and not get scared. I got scared weekly (maybe daily): it was a constant faith battle. I wish I could tell you that I entered His rest and stayed there, but I didn't, and I think it got to a lot of people who tried to join, waiting for God to break through. Or maybe God just called them away for something else He was doing. I don't know.

Phil left in a weird way, but I'm not God, so I don't know what was going on in his heart or in his life. After Phil left, a partner company also left, so we couldn't do low-voltage wiring anymore. Just as fast, we were back to just computer-network services, "keyboard dusting," Andre B. called it.

Andre was great: he came along with a big heart and great business, technical and especially analytical skills. He has an MBA, and he used to work for PriceWaterhouseCoopers in New York. He could spreadsheet anything in twenty seconds and start tracking and analyzing to make decisions based on data. He was lightning.

When a company claimed to be able to help us raise funding, Andre went to work on their contract, finding out that it laid most of the work on us using our friends and family. That's not what we needed. We later worked on IT services (keyboard dusting) and software projects with Andre N. (more on him soon).

DO YOU BELIEVE?

In 2007, while I had some used part-broken desks for the keyboard dusting (computer & networking services company) and the ministry, I advertised and prayed for a part-time technical support technician. That's when the other Andre answered that call, even though he was director of IT at a ministry. I told him about the vision of Alpha Fiber and Alpha World Ministries, and he said, "I'll take it!" I said, "What? Why would you take a part-time technician's job as a director of IT with a master's degree?" He said, "Because God told my wife and me to leave that job, and we believe this is where He wants us next."

Miracle 88. Andre N. joins both Alpha Fiber and Alpha World Ministries, even though I barely have part-time work for him.

Andre had great skills in ministry technologies, and in no time, he enabled us to have a website with ministry videos up and running. As we prayed about which videos would be most helpful to people and which ones God wanted us to start with, I felt like God said to start at the beginning (of course!): Do you believe?

So, we prayed and asked other people to start praying, and I started to formulate a cohesive group of messages based on the doubts I answered with my own research and questioning. I pulled out the many books, continued praying, and began. I was planning to put this first section on the website, followed by other topics that God illuminates in the Bible, but then I felt like God said, "Do it outside."

Huh, *outside?* What? I was sensing that the Lord wanted me to communicate this at some outside venue. *I must not have heard You right,* I thought. *I'm just planning on putting up a video on a website. I don't have time to plan a big event.* I really wanted to sort of put my fingers in my ears and shout, "La, la, la, la, I can't hear you; I can't hear you." But I eventually surrendered, "If You, Lord, will do it, I'll walk it out." (Just like the Sunday school class message with no preparation: if you'll do it, I'll move my lips!)

I prayed and asked the Lord to confirm it by giving me the vision for it, and He did: at a venue, with people praying in one-color T-shirts for the people who are listening. With tables for all the community churches so the churches would be immediately available to any person who "opened the door when Jesus knocked." People delivering the messages, but in between, there is music to bring people closer to the Lord.

I really didn't want to undertake another big thing, but I prayed that the Lord confirm it again. Think: now make the fleece *wet* and all around it *dry*. Go, Gideon! (Judges 6:39). I asked the Lord to confirm it again by giving me the music and favor since I had no money, knowing God could make a way through that impossible hurdle.

When I ended that confirmation request prayer with "Amen," Joey Ebach came to mind. He was the worship leader at our church, and he had a Christian band. So, I called him on the phone.

I said, "Hey, Joey, I feel like God is calling me to do this event outdoors for Him, and I want to see if you and your band would be interested."

He said, "Tell me more."

I told him, "A Do You Believe event to go through the truths that people can know so that they have the evidence to believe in Jesus and make their own decision. A talking-heads format, with music in between. We don't have any money right now, so I can't promise any money."

"We'll do it!"

"How much do you need?"

"Free!" Joey said.

"What?" Why?" I was still secretly hoping not to have to do this!

Joey said, "We've been praying about what God wants to do next for the band, and this sounds just like what we were hearing."

Miracle 89. Joey and the band agree to play for free, and God thereby confirms He will pull together this Do You Believe event.

I knew a lot more needed to fall into place for the event to happen, so we began to pray more about this. And one of the first things we did was enlist other people to commit to pray for this event. As God pulled together the outline (He always does that in me) for this project, the wisdom He provided was to get leaders in each category (this is, of course, good project management). Our prayer leader was Hollie N., and she was awesome. She was tasked with praying (duh), inviting others to join her prayer team to pray for the identified needs of the event as things unfolded, and identifying a specific salvation/prayer needs prayer team (for praying with people at the event).

We had nineteen categories for leaders: speakers, music, artwork, venue, partner churches, promotion, children's leader, setup/takedown, etc. We didn't get a leader for all of them: I'm certain God likes to do that, so we don't ever think "I got this" without thinking, *I got this because He is here, He is in this, and He is doing this!* But with the team God pulled together, we had what we needed (because He…you know).

This is what happens when people of faith join their faith together. I have to reiterate that Andre and his wife felt led to leave his previous paying position as director of IT for a ministry without knowing where God would send him. They had to pray, fast, and trust God that by faith, they would hear from Him. Andre had to, by faith, take the job at Alpha Fiber as a part-time technician to join in what God was doing at Alpha World Ministries.

Since my wife and I were, by faith, continuing to trust that we were hearing from God correctly in taking time away from keyboard dusting to do a Do You Believe event, the collision of our faith with Andre and his wife's faith, and the many, many others that joined in, resulted in powerful moves of God.

One of the moves of God toward this event was the pulling together of the topics and the speakers. As I prayed about what the Lord wanted to say and who He wanted to speak, I felt like God said to answer three simple questions:

1. *Is there a God?* Answer: yes, look up and look in. Meaning: look up at the universe and all that He has created and ordered. And look inside the human body! I was using a book I read by Dr. James P. Gills called *God's Prescription for Healing*, and in it, he points out when we have a paper cut, there are a bunch of processes that take place. I mean a bunch; here's what Dr. Gills says in that book:

> *When we cut a finger, for example, there is an immensely complex response for repair in each cell in the area of the injury. Through an elaborate cascade of reactions, protein messages are sent and received. Vessels are narrowed accordingly, protective scabs are constructed, and cell duplication for the regeneration of new flesh begins. This involves thousands and thousands of individual reactions amongst the trillions of atoms that make up the cells around the wound site. It is a process of unfathomable complexity, mystery, and mastery.[6]*

What? Did you hear that? Thousands of reactions are programmed into our human bodies to take place for just a paper cut!

2. The second question we would present is: *Who is the real God?* Answer: He is Jesus! There is so much evidence that Jesus died on the cross and rose again after being dead to allow anyone and everyone to have a way to be reconciled to God. *The Case for Easter* had three small chapters, and the *Case for Christ* covered over ten different categories of evidence that Lee Strobel studied to try and disprove Christianity!

3. And the third question: *What else do we know about Him?* Answer: everything that the descendants of Abraham, Isaac, and Jacob (Israel) did, all the feasts and festivals, all the laws and the prophets—all pointed to Jesus. He is the Jewish Messiah that they are waiting for, and He is the sacrificial Lamb, like the one they slay every year on the day of atonement to atone or wash away their sins for the year. One of the books here was from Stan Telchin, called *Betrayed! How Do You Feel When You Are Successful, 50, and Jewish, and Your 21-Year-Old Daughter Tells*

---

[6] James P. Gills, *God's Prescription for Healing* (Lake Mary: Charisma Media, 2004), XVIII.

You She Believes in Jesus? Stan talks about that subtitle and all the things that convinced him that Jesus is the Jewish Messiah and the living God of all. By the way, Stan also set out to disprove Christianity because he wanted his daughter back!

What was even more amazing was what happened next. God said, "Have the people in your book speak at the event for each of the three questions!"

Now, I knew Dr. Gills a little bit from church. He attended the Bible study, and he and his wife worshipped at that church too. He also spoke from the pulpit at times, as Pastor Herb felt led to bring him up to speak. But the others—I didn't know them from Adam!

I said, "Lord, do You want me to invite Lee Strobel and Stan Telchin and Dr. Gills?" And I felt like God instead wanted me to invite the man Lee Strobel went to see in the "prove to me He was dead" part of his book. His name is Dr. Alexander Metherell.

I alerted the prayer team, and we began to pray in earnest for God to just make a way. There didn't seem to be any way at all that these people would be willing and available. I mean: here I am, I'm a nobody, with a fledgling computer-services company (no more fiber bids at the moment, no more low voltage/smart home wiring at the moment, and no more security wiring at the moment), with a tiny ministry, in a tiny city in Florida, with no previous ministry events. Who would accept that invitation?

But God (there it is again) had already orchestrated things months ago. I knew Dr. Gills a little, and his admin wasn't sure of how long it would take for him to reply to me, but when I talked to him and his wife at church, he said, "Yes, I'll be there."

But Dr. Metherell, I didn't even know where he lived! When I looked him up, I found out he was on the board of directors for a ministry in Atlanta called Reasons to Believe! Yes, the same people I met while I was in Atlanta. I called them and invited Dr. Metherell, and he said yes! By faith, he was coming to serve the God of the universe.

Miracle 90. God prepares the connections in Atlanta in advance (while going to see a fiber-for-the-kingdom company), and Dr. Metherell accepts the invitation.

When I called about Stan Telchin, I was told he was already traveling the day before and not likely to be available the next day. So, I brought the Metherell success and the Telchin need to the prayer team. By faith, they prayed for the mountain to move, and it did move! It turned out Stan would be in Florida near his home the evening before the event and would be able to drive up that next day for the event.

Miracle 91. Even though already traveling the day before, Stan Telchin is available and accepts our invitation to speak.

There were many more miracles, as you might imagine, for a person with no real salary, a struggling one-man business (Andre soon felt called to go out west with his wife to minister), and a tiny ministry to try and achieve, but with God, all things are possible (Matthew 19:26).

The next few years got even more interesting (if that's at all possible!). In 2010, I founded an alternative-energy company after learning and then teaching alternative-energy classes. On a trip to get other employees trained, the Lord poured out the wisdom for five patents to three of us while we were driving: myself and two colleagues I hired for the alternative-energy company.

Miracle 92!

From there, I felt a strong call to join the ministry called Campsite Ministries, which was under Dr. Joe John. We rented our house and moved into an RV (initially in Gary and Fran's driveway) to minister to people in RV parks. But shortly after, the Lord had me go right back to work as a sales and operations manager for another local company. He gave me the wisdom to succeed there even as I helped a woman who needed to draw closer to the Father.

All along, I was still very immersed in technology, especially communications. My early design engineering was in communications; some of my classes toward my master's degree in electrical engineering (which I never finished) were communications focused, and of course, the fiber-communications-service-provider company that I founded was constantly reevaluating WiMAX, Wi-Fi, next-generation cellular, DWDM, and many other technologies.

So, when the Lord directed me to continue in technology, it was not unusual to me. What was unusual was that, even though I had been out of the semiconductor field directly for longer than is usually accepted, I was now right back in the semiconductor field. In fact, with experience in products, computers, servers, IT services, smart-home technology, alternative energy, and communications services, I had experience in many areas that Intel was selling semiconductors into. So, when God opens a door, no man can shut it!

In 2014, we moved to Hillsboro, Oregon, and the Lord continued to bless us and restore our finances in a miraculous fashion as I worked for Intel and followed what God said regarding finances. He restored all that "the locusts had eaten," and then some! And God will continue to do that. His hundredfold will not fail because His Word says so. Stay tuned for that update from me later!

Back to 2008: the Do You Believe 2008 event took place in Clearwater Coachman Park, the day before Easter that year. After all the prayers and the work, all the planning, all the advertising, including a TV ad, it rained that day all day. It seemed to be a total washout.

Very few people came that day, even though the park could hold ten thousand people. I remember cleaning everything up, and with almost everyone gone, I sat there looking at the park through a rainy windshield in my car. I prayed, "All that work, Lord!" That's all I could say. I was almost overwhelmed. Then the Lord answered by sending one of His servants. Pastor Fred Ball suddenly drove up in his car. He was supposed to be there but was running late, he told me. I think he could see from my face, and from the weather report, that this was less than stellar. Pastor Ball had allowed me to preach a message on believing at his church in Clearwater, as did a few others after we prayed about and discussed what God was doing. So, Pastor Ball knew some of what went into that event. I think I said, "Not a great turnout." And he said, "You know, Rich, the Lord would do the whole thing, even if it was just to save one!"

Then I remembered: one guy came up at the end and said to me, "I understood everything that man said [referring to Dr. Alexander Metherell]." This was amazing since you almost need a master's degree just to listen to Dr. Metherell speak: he's that smart! This guy continued, "And I used to think that my science was at odds with my faith, but now I know that it is not. So, thank you!"

Wow! God, in His great love, would even set up this whole event for just one person. He says He would leave the ninety-nine to go get the lost one! In Matthew 18:12–14, Jesus described how the Father strives to find the one:

What do you think? If a man owns a hundred sheep, and one of them wanders away, will he not leave the ninety-nine on the hills and go to look for the one that wandered off? And if he finds it, truly I tell you, he is happier about that one sheep than about the ninety-nine that did not wander off. In the same way your Father in heaven is not willing that any of these little ones should perish.

And again, in Luke 15:1–7:

Now the tax collectors and sinners were all gathering around to hear Jesus. But the Pharisees and the teachers of the law muttered, "This man welcomes sinners and eats with them."

Then Jesus told them this parable: "Suppose one of you has a hundred sheep and loses one of them. Doesn't he leave the ninety-nine in the open country and go after the lost sheep until he finds it? And when he finds it, he joyfully puts it on his shoulders and goes home. Then he calls his friends and neighbors together and says, 'Rejoice with me; I have found my lost sheep.' I tell you that in the same way there will be more rejoicing in heaven over one sinner who repents than over ninety-nine righteous persons who do not need to repent."

Is all of this reaching your heart? These are spiritual matters, so you have to step into the spiritual realm to perceive these truths. Stick your head out the metaphorical window into the great spiritual world, beyond what you can just see. Not just to make-believe stuff or lies but to overwhelmingly proven items of God's presence and love for everyone.

The thing I'd like to end with is this: when Jesus was walking by, two blind men called out to receive their sight, and He gave it to them, fulfilling Isaiah 35:5: "Then the eyes of the blind will be opened. And the ears of the deaf will be unstopped."

But before Jesus gave them their sight, He asked them the most important question on this whole planet. He asked them, "Do you believe I am able to do this?" And they said, "Yes, Lord." And He said, "Then, by your faith, it is done to you." That's your most important question too. And Jesus is asking you, "Do you believe?"

Bibliography

Behe, Michael J. *Darwin's Black Box* (second edition). Free Press, 2006.

Blackaby, Henry T. and Claude V. King. *Experiencing God*. Lifeway Christian Resources, 1990.

Chan, Francis. *Crazy Love*. David C. Cook, 2008.

Christian Broadcasting Network. "Biblical Prophecies Fulfilled by Jesus." Accessed November 30, 2021. https://www1.cbn.com/biblestudy/biblical-prophecies-fulfilled-by-jesus.

Cymbala, Jim. *When God's People Pray*. Zondervan, 2007.

Gills, James P. *God's Prescription for Healing. Five Divine Gifts of Healing*. Charisma Media, 2004.

Keller, Timothy. *The Reason for God*. Penguin Publishing Group, 2009.

Lewis, Clive Staples. *Mere Christianity*. Simon & Schuster, 1986.

Mackie, J. L. *The Miracle of Theism*. Oxford, 1982.

McDowell, Josh and Sean McDowell. *Evidence That Demands a Verdict. Life-Changing Truth for a Skeptical World*. Thomas Nelson, 2017.

McDowell, Josh. *Evidence That Demands a Verdict. Historical Evidences for the Christian Faith* (previous version). Thomas Nelson, 1979.

Moore, Beth, *Jesus the One and Only*. Lifeway Christian Resources, 2000.

Moore, Beth. *Daniel: Lives of Integrity, Words of Prophecy*. Lifeway Christian Resources, 2006.

Müller, George. *The Autobiography of George Müller*. Whitaker House, 1996.

Stanley, Andy. *Visioneering*. Doubleday Religious Publishing Group, 1999.

Stott, John. *Basic Christianity*. Wm. B. Eerdmans Publishing Company, 1959.

Strobel, Lee. *The Case for Christ. A Journalist's Personal Investigation of the Evidence for Jesus. Updated and Expanded*. Zondervan, 2016.

Strobel, Lee. *The Case for Christ. A Journalist's Personal Investigation of the Evidence for Jesus* (previous version). Zondervan, 1998.

Strobel, Lee. *The Case for Easter. A Journalist Investigates the Evidence for the Resurrection*. Zondervan, 2003.

Swindoll, Chuck. Insight for Living Ministries. Accessed November 30, 2021. www.insight.org.

Telchin, Stan. *Betrayed! How Do You Feel When You Are Successful, 50, and Jewish, and Your 21-Year-Old Daughter Tells You She Believes in Jesus?* Zondervan, 1983.

Wilkinson, Bruce. *Prayer of Jabez*. Multnomah, 2001.

Wilkinson, Bruce. *You Were Born for This* (reprint). Multnomah, 2011.

Author's Bio

Rich Mason has an electrical engineering degree from the University of South Florida and has been in technology and business for thirty-seven years, founding three startups and multiple provisional patents. He has served in numerous ministry capacities, including founding Alpha World Ministries, which did the original Do You Believe event, chairing the council in the Tarpon Springs church his family and he attended, leading small groups and Bible studies, organizing hurricane relief, among other serving positions.

After starting college in Brooklyn, NY, and then finishing in the Tampa, Florida, area, he and his family felt led to the Pacific Northwest to Hillsboro, Oregon, where they currently divide their time between both states. He and his wife of thirty-four years have three grown children and are praying for grandkids.

CPSIA information can be obtained
at www.ICGtesting.com
Printed in the USA
BVHW031301230622
640493BV00014B/1159